Ashes to Ashes

Ashes to Ashes

Mourning and Social Difference in F. Scott Fitzgerald's Fiction

Jonathan Schiff

SUP

Selinsgrove: Susquehanna University Press
London: Associated University Presses

Associated University Presses
440 Forsgate Drive
Cranbury, NJ 08512

Associated University Presses
16 Barter Street
London WC1A 2AH, England

Associated University Presses
P.O. Box 338, Port Credit
Mississauga, Ontario
Canada L5G 4L8

The paper used in this publication meets the requirements of the American National Standard for Permanence of Paper for Printed Library Materials Z39.48-1984.

Library of Congress Cataloging-in-Publication Data

Schiff, Jonathan, 1967–
    Ashes to ashes : mourning and social difference in F. Scott Fitzgerald's fiction / Jonathan Schiff.
        p.   cm.
    Includes bibliographical references (p.   ) and index.
    ISBN 1-57591-046-2 (alk. paper)
    1. Fitzgerald, F. Scott (Francis Scott), 1896–1940—Knowledge—Psychology.   2. Fitzgerald, F. Scott (Francis Scott), 1896–1940—Political and social views.   3. Psychological fiction, American—History and criticism.   4. Difference (Psychology) in literature.   5. Mourning customs in literature.   6. Social classes in literature.   I. Title.
    PS3511.I9 Z837   2001
    813'.52—dc21   00-57334

For my grandfather, Samuel Shapiro
and my mother, Dorothy Schiff Shannon

"The excursion is the same when you go looking for your sorrow as when you go looking for your joy," said Doc.

—Eudora Welty, "The Wide Net"

Contents

Acknowledgments

My foremost debts are to Jeffrey Berman and Jennifer Fleischner. Jeff helped me to remain vigilant toward countertransference issues, while Jennifer helped me to go beyond my psychoanalytic focus by expanding into cultural and literary areas. Their other contributions to this project are too numerous to mention.

I am appreciative of Hans Feldmann, Director of Susquehanna University Press, as well as the Board of Directors at the Press, for their faith in my project. I am also appreciative of the anonymous outsider reader who provided encouraging comments.

I would like to thank Vamik D. Volkan, M.D. for reading and commenting on both my early findings and completed manuscript.

I have also received helpful information or advice along the way from Cailin Brown, Carl Eby, Fred Silva, Robert Trogdon, and the St. Paul, Minnesota Department of Vital Statistics.

The photograph on the cover of this book is part of the F. Scott Fitzgerald Papers; Manuscripts Division; Department of Rare Books and Special Collections; Princeton University Library. Anna Lee Pauls, of the Princeton University Library, was very helpful in answering my many questions.

Extracts of Fitzgerald's works, including *The Great Gatsby* and *Tender Is the Night,* are reprinted by permission of Harold Ober Associates Incorporated.

In addition, extracts from *The Great Gatsby* ("Authorized Text") are reprinted with permission of Scribner, a Division of Simon & Schuster, from *The Great Gatsby* ("Authorized Text") by F. Scott Fitzgerald. Copyright 1925 by Charles Scribner's Sons. Copyright renewed 1953 by Frances Scott Fitzgerald Lanahan. Copyright © 1991, 1992 by Eleanor Lanahan, Matthew Bruccoli, and Samuel J. Lanahan as Trustees under Agreement Date July 3, 1975, created by Frances Scott Fitzgerald Smith.

In addition, extracts from *Tender Is the Night* are reprinted with permission of Scribner, a Division of Simon & Schuster, from *Tender Is the Night* by F. Scott Fitzgerald. Copyright, 1933, 1934 by Charles Scribner's Sons. Copyrights renewed © 1961, 1962 by Frances Scott Fitzgerald Lanahan.

Introduction

IN THIS STUDY, I EXPLORE HOW THE EXPERIENCE OF SIBLING LOSS contributed to F. Scott Fitzgerald's literary career. I suggest that Fitzgerald wrote about a constellation of various mourning patterns from his childhood: his parents' alternate preoccupation with grief for his two elder sisters and displacement of their grief onto him, behavior that in turn encouraged his sense of maternal and paternal loss, but also his identification with their grief. Furthermore, these circumstances contributed to his literary insights into cultural mourning norms. Previous critics sharing my psychoanalytic interest have explored only one of these forms of mourning—maternal loss—in Fitzgerald's fiction.[1] In investigating all of these forms of mourning, I draw in particular upon an assortment of psychoanalytic theorists, including John Bowlby, Sigmund Freud, Melanie Klein, Heinz Kohut, Vamik D. Volkan, and D. W. Winnicott.

This study contradicts a perspective on Fitzgerald provided in *The Literary History of the United States*: "What is certain . . . is that he could never come to grips with the central inner conflict in his writing, and he moved to his outward and cultural studies of the American financial aristocracy at the cost of suppressing rather than resolving the problem."[2] Not only did Fitzgerald examine a central inner conflict in writing about his parents' grief for his sisters, but he also confronted his feelings about that conflict in turning to "his outward and cultural studies." The psychological and cultural aspects of his fiction are related, each aspect helping to explain the other. His upbringing among parents preoccupied with grief is linked with his literary portrayals of economic, ethnic, and racial outsiders—three of the types of social difference alluded to in the subtitle of this study—who struggle to receive acceptance in a society where insiders are consumed with nostalgia for a more aristocratic America and are resistant to change.

13

In addition, in writing about his personal experiences with mourning, Fitzgerald pointed out his society's construction of gender, the final type of social difference alluded to in the subtitle of this study. His fiction vividly illustrates the cultural opposition between masculinity and mourning, what Pamela Boker has referred to as the American "grief taboo." Boker analyzes the repressed sense of maternal loss that surfaces in the fiction of Herman Melville, Mark Twain, and Ernest Hemingway. Noting that her study is not meant to be all-inclusive, she sees these male writers' resistance to grief as characteristic of American culture as a whole.[3] While Fitzgerald demonstrates an anxiety over violating that grief taboo, he eventually overcomes that anxiety in two ways: first, by portraying in a positive light those male characters who express their grief and who identify or consciously empathize with others' grief, and second, by parodying male characters who repress or deny feelings of loss. Every one of his novels, including his final unfinished one, hinges upon one or both of these two narrative strategies.

In effect, this study complicates two justifiably influential views of Fitzgerald's fiction. In noting Fitzgerald's tendency to conceal hostility toward female characters by idealizing them, Leslie Fiedler and Judith Fetterley have both revealed an antifeminist element in Fitzgerald's fiction.[4] On the one hand, I add further support to that view in my analysis of his tendency to displace anger toward his grieving mother onto many of his female characters. On the other hand, I suggest that in his literary efforts to identify with his grieving parents, validating those gender roles that are marginalized in a patriarchal society and critiquing those that are privileged, Fitzgerald imbues his writing with an implicitly feminist element.[5] A feminist discussion, I feel, should take into account both the antifeminist and feminist elements in his fiction.

CHAPTER SYNOPSES

Chapter 1 provides a fresh biographical perspective, a discussion of the importance of sibling loss in Fitzgerald's life, an event that prior biographers have not explored in depth. While Fitzgerald has been portrayed as the child of doting parents, I suggest that his parents' doting behavior masked their chronic, underlying grief. I further suggest that though their preoccupation encouraged his self-absorption and self-destructiveness, it also promoted an opposing empathic side to his personality. In the subsequent chapters of this study, I draw upon this biographical perspective in order to illuminate Fitzgerald's writings. In chapter 2, I allude to Fitzgerald's ambivalence toward his grieving mother in order to point out the captious and hostile views of motherhood expressed in some of Fitzgerald's stories. However, the chapter also analyzes "The Ice Palace" as Fitzgerald's endorsement of feminist values, a viewpoint fostered by his identification with "feminine" grief and counteridentification with "masculine" repressiveness. Chapter 3, on *This Side of Paradise*, links Amory's difficulty in progressing into maturity with his upbringing in a society where people place a blind faith in Victorian progress and resist the work of mourning. Ultimately, Amory matures by learning to grieve, identifying with his father's romantic ("masculine") and his mother's sentimental ("feminine") modes of mourning—crosscurrents of grief within the dominant culture. Chapter 4, on *The Beautiful and Damned*, provides an examination of Anthony's attraction-repulsion to the work of mourning, including his ambivalence toward the efforts of his wife, his mother-in-law, and other women in general, and his efforts to cope with bereavement by turning to occultism. Fitzgerald's interest in the occult, which I further explore in subsequent chapters, has received scant attention. The chapter also suggests that after being raised by adults preoccupied with grief, Anthony projects his self-ambivalent sense of familial otherness onto a social outsider—the Jewish character Joseph Bloeckman. In the discussion of *The Great Gatsby* in chapter 5, I suggest that the novel's theme of oral aggression is related to Fitzgerald's resentment of his mother's preoccupation with grief. Daisy Buchanan and several other characters remain in a frozen state of mourning, ambivalent toward minorities seeking change, such as Gatz / Gatsby. These grieving characters displace their emotions onto objects to such a degree that death becomes a commodity in their modern world. Expressions of grief surface only in brief bursts, as in Daisy's behavior and in Myrtle's party, a symbolic seance that leaves Nick feeling effeminized. Despite the depictions of Daisy and Myrtle, however, the novel ultimately validates "feminine" mourning through its portrayal of Gatsby's grief for Daisy and Nick's grief for Gatsby. Chapter 6 provides an analysis of a split in Dick Diver's psyche. On the one hand, as the self-perceived "last hope of a decaying clan," he feels compelled to empathize with others' grief, while on the other hand, as a male, he feels he should repress that desire. Consequently, his compulsion emerges in sudden, desperate efforts to rescue others, efforts that lead him to violate the ethics of his psychiatric profession and the vows of his marriage. Rather than attempting to cure Nicole's schizophrenia, he attempts to teach her to cope with loss. In that unconscious goal, he succeeds. Ultimately, however, the split in his psyche develops into hysteria, the "female malady"—what he refers to as "non combatant's shell-shock." In examining the relationship between shell shock and gender roles, Fitzgerald demonstrates insight into an important psychological issue of his time. Chapter 7, the brief, final chapter of this study, analyzes *The Last Tycoon* as Fitzgerald's attempt to work through feelings of bereavement for his estranged wife, Zelda, and daughter, Scottie, a role involving his simultaneous attempt to work through his sense of maternal and paternal loss. Fitzgerald's alter ego, Monroe Stahr, mourns for his dead wife. Meanwhile, Stahr attempts to cope with loss in the world around him. As a Jew of humble origins, he feels concern for working class persons struggling in the depression. At the same time, having achieved wealth and prominence, he "mourns" for an aristocratic past formerly sealed off to him and thus plays the role of paternalistic, Hollywood leader. Stahr envisions the motion picture industry as a unifying force in society. He promotes collaborative film production, and he wishes to make movies that everyone will wish to see. In effect, in a reflection of his creator's literary efforts, he promotes creativity and empathy as important elements in the healing process.

METHODS AND AIMS

Many writers have articulated compelling reasons for the validity and importance of psychobiography, but I will say a few words about my psychoanalytic approach.[6]

While I feel that a significant part of Fitzgerald's accomplishment as an artist consisted of his ability to explore inner conflicts going all the way back to his birth, I recognize that his art consists of other accomplishments. Consequently, I discuss Fitzgerald's art as more than a psychological case study. Throughout the book, I relate Fitzgerald's psychological insights to certain literary and cultural issues, such as the structure of the bildungsroman and cultural attitudes toward mourning.

In addition, in showing how he often responded adaptively by rebelling against normative social roles, I avoid pathologizing the artist and the art. In portraying Fitzgerald as self-destructive, I do not mean to revive the myth that he squandered his talent. Van Gogh was not only self-destructive, but also hard working and disciplined, and Fitzgerald follows that pattern.

Some readers may wonder why I do not focus on differences between the emotions arising from temporary parental loss in infancy and early childhood; permanent parental loss in childhood; and loss in adulthood. One reason I do not do so is because I am influenced by Bowlby's exhaustively researched work on mourning. Bowlby repeatedly stresses the similarities in individuals' responses to all of these forms of loss.[7] Another reason I do not discuss differences in the emotions surrounding different experiences of loss is that I do not perceive any lines of demarcation in Fitzgerald's fiction. What is important about these different forms of loss in Fitzgerald's fiction is the conflict arising when characters grieving for different reasons come into contact with each other—for example, when Gatsby, displaying maternal loss, reacts to Daisy's sense of loss surrounding the birth of her daughter.

My interpretation raises a question for readers to consider further. What should we consider more important in a feminist reading—Fitzgerald's mother-blaming tendency, or his anti-patriarchal depiction of society's gender roles? My interpretation also implicitly raises related questions, ones that can never be fully answered. To what extent can or should we resolve our sense of loss and put the past behind us? To what extent does the past exist in the present? Both psychoanalysis and Fitzgerald's fiction deepen our appreciation of these mysteries.

Ashes to Ashes

1

"Edge of a Precipice": Fitzgerald as a Changeling for the Dead

Mrs. Smith had been born on the edge of an imaginary prec-
ipice and had lived there ever since, looking over the preci-
pice every half hour in horror and yet unable to get herself
away.

—*The Notebooks of F. Scott Fitzgerald*

Well, three months before i was born," fitzgerald writes
in his autobiographical essay "An Author's House" (1936), "my
mother lost her other two children and I think that came first
of all though I don't know how it worked exactly. I think I
started then to be a writer."[1] Fitzgerald's biographers have not
explored at length "how it worked."[2] Yet Fitzgerald felt a need
to return to the issue, for he had twice before referred to the
two losses—in a passage of his posthumously published essay
"The Death of My Father," and in a revised version of that passage in *Tender Is the Night* (1933).

In requesting and receiving copies of the sisters' death cer-
tificates and obituaries from the city of St. Paul, Minnesota, I
have learned that Fitzgerald was correct about the date of one
elder sister's death. The eldest sister, Louise, died on 13 June
1896, at the age of three after an illness, a date that indeed fell
about three months before his birth on 24 September of that
year. However, the second eldest sister, Mary Ashton, died on
25 November 1895, at the age of seventeen months, also after
an illness. The mere ten-month gap between that date and Fitzgerald's birth indicates the strong possibility that he was deliberately conceived as a substitute for her. Certainly the eldest
sister was seen as Francis Scott's direct precursor, since as her
death certificate and obituary indicate, her middle name had

also been Scott. While Fitzgerald's biographers have noted
that his parents provided a hint of their ambitions for him
when they named him after his ancestor Francis Scott Key, the
composer of "The Star Spangled Banner," they have not explored the implications surrounding their decision to name
him after a much closer relative.

I will posit here that Fitzgerald's parents' unresolved grief
severely complicated their relationship with him. In doting
upon him, they unsuccessfully masked an inner desire to withdraw from him, to grieve for the sisters. Fitzgerald, in turn,
wavered throughout his life between a desire to serve as familial rescuer and a resistance to that role. Such behavior encouraged his self-destructiveness but also fostered his exuberant,
creative efforts to transgress normative gender roles and accept the culturally unmanly role of empathizing with others'
grief.

THE "REPLACEMENT CHILD," OR THE "LIVING LINKING OBJECT"

Before turning to an analysis of Fitzgerald's life, we can benefit from a brief psychoanalytic discussion. In citing the following theories and case histories, I do not mean to suggest
that they permit us to draw immediate conclusions about Fitzgerald's life. Biographical evidence will be necessary. However, these theories and case histories will help us to be on the
lookout for certain patterns in Fitzgerald's life. And we can
later be on the lookout for textual evidence of similar patterns
in the lives of his characters.

We may begin with Freud, who has explored the "uncanny,"
the sense of alienation, fear, and dread that comes upon many
of us, for example, when we read certain works of fiction.
Freud finds that the "uncanny is really nothing new or alien
but something which is familiar and old-established in the
mind and which has become alienated from it only through the
process of repression."[3] The uncanny was familiar to us at a
period in our earliest infancy, that of primary narcissism, when
we are unable to distinguish between self and other. At this
stage, we experience a feeling of "omnipotence of thoughts," in

which no object exists independently from us. In other words, the "other" is our double and serves as "insurance against the destruction of the ego."[4] However, as we mature, leaving this stage of omnipotence, the "double reverses its aspect. From having been an assurance of immortality, it becomes the uncanny harbinger of death."[5] Since an element of narcissism continues to play a role in the minds of adults, the double in literature and other harbingers of death, such as dead bodies and ghosts, often produce conflicting feelings of unfamiliarity and familiarity, fear and omnipotence.

Freud's theory suggests that a child raised as a substitute for a deceased sibling would be particularly prone to uncanny feelings. As long as the parents display feelings of grief, the child is reminded of his or her double—the deceased sibling. The literature on the "replacement child" furthers our insight into the surviving sibling's situation. In 1964, Albert C. Cain and Barbara S. Cain coined the terms "replacement child" and "substitute child" to refer to a child whom the parents conceive shortly after losing another child. Sometimes a child is conceived expressly for the purpose. However, the parents' guilt over the first child's death typically inhibits resolution of the mourning process. Moreover, often the parents' narcissistic investment in the deceased child further inhibits resolution, for with the child's death, all the parents' "identifications, dreams, and plans" die too. Fearing that the new child will also die young, the parents often overprotect him or her. However, the parents also typically feel an opposing desire to withdraw from the replacement child, focusing instead on the dead child, who is often idealized. Frequently, the parents accidentally call the new child by the dead child's name. Moreover, they frequently find themselves comparing the replacement child's appearance and mannerisms with those of the dead child, even if the two children are of different sexes. In addition, the Cains find, the parents sometimes unconsciously displace their self-reproaches onto the replacement child, envisioning him or her as responsible for the other child's death. Attempting to explain how a replacement child, still unborn, can be blamed by the parents for the death, the Cains write that the

timelessness, facile displacements, obliviousness to contradictions, and unreason of the unconscious know no . . . boundaries of logic and reality. At best we can reconstruct the unconscious content and articulate it in secondary-process [unconscious] language it runs something like the following. "This new child is alive *instead* of our dead child. He has *taken his place*. This child is not our dead child, he was to be, it is his fault he is not. It isn't fair that he should live and our other child die. He is responsible for *all* this, it is *all his fault*."[6]

The parents' anxiety-ridden parenting encourages the replacement child to suffer from intense phobias, to experience physical symptoms formerly experienced by the deceased, and to fear that he or she will die young, as did the elder sibling. This fear of death recalls Freud's theory about the uncanny nature of the double, its role as a harbinger of death. The replacement child's phobic nature may also arise from an expectation of punishment from the parents, when they have displaced blame onto him or her. Furthermore, the parents' preoccupation with an idealized, deceased child encourages the replacement child to see that child as a competitor. The replacement child's despair and "inexpressible rage" over the constant explicit and implicit comparisons with the competitor is often internalized, a process that manifests itself through "abortive negative identities and vengeful school failures."[7]

Elva Orlow Poznanski has further examined the situation. Poznanski writes of a 15-year-old girl, Susie, who acquired a "past history" serving as a replacement for an idealized deceased sister. Susie had a sense of failing to fulfill her father's lofty expectations for her in scholastics and other areas. Moreover, she demonstrated a pattern of self-destructiveness, including a suicide attempt and involvement with three different boyfriends who had been in trouble with the police. One of these boyfriends tried to kill her. Echoing the Cains, Poznanski stresses the important role that the idealization of the dead child appears to have played in the patient's lack of self-regard and self-destructiveness. Parents idealize the dead child, she proposes, in order to stave off feelings of anger toward the deceased. And the parents further avoid the emotions surrounding the loss by turning to the replacement child. They are thus able "partially to deny the first child's death. The replacement child then acts as a barrier to the parental acknowledgment of death, since a real child exists who is a substitute."[8]

Vamik D. Volkan formulates a metapsychological theory providing us with further insight into the predicament of the replacement child from the replacement child's point of view. He refers to the replacement child as a "living linking object." The "linking object," either an inanimate or animate one, serves as an "embodied meeting ground" between the mourner and the deceased loved one. Volkan stresses that unlike mourners who cherish mementos of the deceased, those mourners who adopt linking objects keep them out of sight, turning to them only occasionally. Consequently, the linking object provides them with a sense that they are able to preserve or "kill" the individual they have lost. The objects thus facilitate the freezing of the mourning process, since mourners are able to "distance themselves" from their ambivalence toward the deceased. Often the mourners do not comprehend why the linking object is important to them, experiencing instead a feeling of eeriness in its presence. Volkan refers to the use of linking objects as a pathological response to mourning. His assertion accords with the work of John Bowlby, who views "chronic mourning"—the avoidance of grief in favor of the belief that the loss is reversible—as one form of pathological mourning. We see a demonstration of chronic mourning in the individual who confronts grief only intermittently through the use of the linking object.[9]

Volkan cites numerous cases in which patients had adopted a linking object. I will summarize one case in order to provide a sharper sense of how the linking object, unlike the typical memento of the deceased, can foster the freezing of the mourning process. Volkan writes of a patient who transferred her feelings toward her estranged father onto her former psychiatrist. When she voiced concern that that psychiatrist was depressed, he denied it. Before a subsequent session, she learned that he had hanged himself, and her appointment card for that session became a linking object. She put it in an urn and placed the urn atop her living room mantel. For three years, she never removed or looked at it. Despite or because of this attempt to distance herself from her grief, she continued to remain in mourning for him. She often attempted to keep her missed appointment with him by parking her car in his office lot. She sought out a new psychiatrist only when her husband, unhappy with her preoccupation with the deceased psychiatrist, left her.[10]

The *living* linking object, Volkan explains, is seen as a "meeting place" between the parent's self-image and the parent's image of the dead person. The living linking object thus inherits a "psychological gene." How exactly is that gene passed on? Volkan cites numerous psychoanalysts who have observed the existence of an "affective flow" between mother and child. He compares the process to the "conveying of infection by the transmission of germs."[11] Living linking objects acquire not only a "past history," as Poznanski put it, but they also develop a feeling of "generational continuity," even a sense of immortality. This sense of immortality recalls an aspect of the Freudian uncanny, in which the double initially serves as assurance against the destruction of the ego. For Volkan, living linking objects must learn to integrate those traits that link them to the grieving parent and dead person with those they feel are uniquely their own. "Some children make this adaptation in ways that from a social point of view are seen as creative, but others respond to the situation in ways that from a clinical viewpoint are seen as 'crazy.' "[12] Thus, while the Cains had mentioned the possibility of adaptation, Volkan's work makes it easier for us to examine the replacement child's situation beyond a "syndrome-like" perspective. In Volkan's view, the living linking object can transform the experience into a healthful one.

In what specific ways have particular living linking objects discussed in Volkan's writings responded to their situation? Volkan has written of a patient, "Frances," who was envisioned as a replacement for her adoptive mother's dead brother. More precisely, she was adopted after her mother miscarried a child whom she had conceived to replace the brother. In addition, after her grandfather died, Frances may have become a replacement for him. Frances described herself as "half dead" and "half alive"; "half female" and "half male." Moreover, she was "obsessed" with Poe's "The Masque of the Red Death" and enjoyed watching movies such as *Night of the Living Dead*, in which dead persons are eaten (introjected). At one point, when Volkan's patient Frances learned of an elderly relative's death, a relative she had never met, she "automatically

assum[ed] her grandmother's attitude toward death."[13] Moreover, she experienced fantasies of rescuing others. We can see
that all of these behaviors suggest an attempt to adapt to her
"psychological gene" as a mourning savior, as a means for reunion between mourner and deceased.

Volkan observes similar rescue fantasies in the life of the
Turkish statesman Kemal Ataturk, who rebelled from his familial role as living linking object but eventually came to fulfill
that role when he achieved legendary status as a savior to his
motherland. In writing of his own role as a replacement for a
deceased uncle, Volkan finds, "the matrix of my choice to become a psychoanalyst may have been my development of early
rescue fantasies."[14]

Other psychoanalytic literature directly or indirectly points
to the predisposition toward rescue fantasies among living linking objects. For evidence, we might consider the life of Thornton Wilder. Jules Glenn has found that Wilder explored rescue
fantasies in his fiction and partially acted on them through his
many compassionate endeavors. Glenn posits that Wilder came
to feel guilt over his stillborn twin brother's death, and his rescue fantasies were encouraged by a desire for atonement.[15] Living linking objects, prone to guilt over the death of the person
they have replaced, would be similarly likely to experience
such a desire. Thus, we can extrapolate a theory of atonement,
a complement to Volkan's theory of the "psychological gene,"
in order to shed light on the replacement child's rescue fantasies.

In fact, George H. Pollock has found the presence of atonement rescue fantasies in the case of Bertha Pappenheim, who
was likely envisioned as a replacement child. Pappenheim was
the "first" patient of psychoanalysis—the young woman referred to as "Anna O" by Josef Breuer and Freud. Breuer began
treating Pappenheim when she took to bed after her father
went through a fatal illness. Pappenheim experienced such
symptoms of illness as muteness and hallucinations. Most of
these symptoms began to disappear as she described them to
Breuer. Reexamining the case history, Pollock finds that her
illness resulted in part from an identification with her dying
father, and in part from identification after his death, and also
in part from guilt over her death wishes toward him. Drawing

upon biographical information, including archival information about the death of a sister before Pappenheim's birth, Pollock further posits that she experienced a form of "survivor
guilt" over her sisters' deaths, and this guilt was one contribut-
ing factor in her intense dedication to her dying father and
pathological reaction to his death. Later in her life, Pollock
notes, she remained especially dedicated to helping others, devoting herself to assisting orphaned Jewish girls.[16]

Bowlby's work further points to the prevalence of rescue
fantasies in living linking objects. Bowlby has discussed the
predisposition toward "compulsive caregiving" among those
who are raised by a sick or depressed parent. While often disre-
garding their own health and emotional well-being, they experience an extreme desire to help the parent, or in later life, a
spouse. Often the caregiver attempts to provide help for those
who do not require it. Bowlby sees a similar proneness toward
compulsive caregiving among those who experienced "intermittent and inadequate" parenting in childhood. In this situation, the caregiver unconsciously identifies with the person
receiving care.[17] We can see that both situations bear relevance
to the lives of living linking objects, since their parents alternately cling to them in order to resolve their grief and withdraw from them as inferiors to the idealized, deceased
children. As an example of compulsive caregiving, Bowlby
cites the case of a boy who devotedly cared for his mother, who
suffered from high blood pressure. She died in adolescence, but
after he finished school, he became "strongly drawn" to a much
older woman who had lived a very "troubled" life. He took it
upon himself to take care of her.[18] Bowlby further writes of a
boy who helped take care of his diabetic mother. He eventually
stayed awake at night and refused to go to school, fearing for
her health.[19]

Drawing upon an account written by Volkan, Bowlby cites
the case of Julia as another example of compulsive caregiving
in an individual who experienced parental deprivation. When
Julia was an infant, her mother was bedridden, and her father
had "taken to drink." As she grew up, her mother was extremely critical of her. As a young adult, Julia turned down
college scholarships in order to take care of her mother, who
was now diabetic. Julia slept by her mother's bed and fre-

quently checked her condition. When she left the house during the day, she would compulsively check on her through repeated telephone calls.[20]

Stanley L. Olinick's work further supports a connection between a child's relationship with a depressed parent and his or her development of rescue fantasies. Drawing upon case histories, which he does not discuss directly for reasons of confidentiality, Olinick has proposed that a "powerful motivation for the psychiatrist dedicating himself to the psychoanalytic relationship is the genetic effect of a rescue fantasy having to do with a depressive mother, the latter having induced such rescue fantasy in her receptive child."[21] Though Olinick focuses on other issues, he briefly elaborates on this point, describing a process that recalls Volkan's reference to the affective flow between mother and child:

The depressive mother in particular has an unwitting but remarkable ability to evoke and induce such fantasies and, in fact, to generate mothering behavior in her child; and this is of course integrated with the child's own developing needs. It is inherent in a relationship founded on mutual dependence, even when one partner is more dominant and the other submissive, that each will expect fulfillment through the other and that what is not actualized externally will be fantasized internally. Thus, the child's developing autonomous ego functions will be pressed into the service of the mothering one. The child will be pressed into becoming the idealized mothering one and into additionally becoming one day the rescuing champion of the distressed woman or man, for the sexualizing and gendering of the rescue motif may cut across and interpenetrate the usual male-female lines."[22]

The relationship between the mourning parent and the living linking object involves just such a "mutual dependence," for the distraught parent relies upon the living linking object to serve as a meeting ground with the beloved deceased person.

Bowlby's work indicates that living linking objects are also prone to reactions of a diametrically opposite nature. Compulsive caregivers, he finds, also frequently demonstrate compulsive self-reliance. Though they strongly desire to help others, they resist accepting the love and support that would help them to cope with their own difficulties. Drawing upon a report by Elizabeth Tuters of the Tavistock clinic in London, Bowlby observes a case of compulsive self-reliance, as well as some evidence of compulsive caregiving, in the life of Visha. When Visha was ten, her father died. Her mother blamed herself for the death, drank "to excess," and felt too upset to take care of Visha. Visha had previously feared inadequate parenting when her father had been alive. Her parents' marriage had been a precarious one, and Visha had felt responsibility for holding the family together. Once her mother had abandoned her when her father had brought home another woman. Now, with her father's death, Visha failed to mourn. Although she betrayed a profound sense of loss, she refused to cry or admit to her unhappiness. She complained that her mother cried too much, and began suffering asthmatic attacks when it was time to attend joint sessions with her mother. Eventually, by drawing emotionally closer to her mother in these sessions, Visha became more able to tolerate her anger and express her sadness.[23] Bowlby cites other cases of compulsive caregiving and self-reliance that are encouraged by inadequate parenting. In the case of the living linking object demonstrating compulsive reliance, we might say that he or she refuses to assimilate the traits of the grieving parent.

Compulsive caregiving and compulsive self-reliance recall the Freudian stage of primary narcissism, in which the child feels a sense of omnipotence. Though Heinz Kohut's theories of narcissism differ from Freud's, his too indicate the narcissistic nature of compulsive self-reliance and compulsive caregiving / rescue fantasizing. Kohut has found that children struggle to progress beyond an early narcissistic stage when they are raised by unempathic parents. This stage involves exhibitionism: in order to receive empathy, the child behaves "grandiosely," clinging to an "unconditional perfection." Kohut describes one patient who grandiosely identified with Christ. He responded to this identification by fantasizing about helping others in the Peace Corps and eventually becoming a minister. Kohut finds that persons who continue to receive underempathy often withdraw in rage. Narcissism does not necessarily lead to pathology, however, according to Kohut. Once tamed, it can promote successes in life, including the development of object love.[24] By extension, then, we might say that the compulsion for caregiving and self-reliance can be tempered to produce beneficial behavior. And to relate Kohut's views directly to Volkan's, we might say that living linking objects must tame their exhibitionistic desire to take on the traits perceived in the parents and the deceased child. They must also tame the desire to withdraw from the parents, to accept only those traits they feel are uniquely their own.

CHRONIC, UNDERLYING GRIEF

In "The Death of My Father," Fitzgerald writes that after his sisters' deaths, his father "felt what the effect of that would be on my mother, that he would be [his son's] only moral guide."[25] Fitzgerald thus implies that his mother was unable to discipline him when he was a child, that in order to compensate for the enormity of her losses, she idealized him. In reality, his father Edward may have idealized him for the same reason. As an adult, Fitzgerald wrote to his cousin Cecilia Taylor: "I was fond of Aunt Annabel and Aunt Elise, who gave me almost my first tastes of discipline."[26] The feminine clothing he wore as an infant would have made it easy for both parents to view him in relation to his sister. As was not uncommon at the time, he was dressed in bloomers, a fact he would record in the portion of his ledger that included an account of significant personal experiences.[27] His straight hair was curled as well, further prettying his fine features. A few years later, as if to reverse the trend and "masculinize" him, Edward encouraged his timid son to box other boys. Since the Fitzgeralds were not affluent, it is possible that he wore his sisters' clothing when he was an infant, and probable that he shared at least one item, such as a crib, that had initially been purchased for them. And for both parents, it would be difficult not to transfer the extreme feelings for the daughters onto the son who shared one daughter's name. He was always called Scott; never Francis or Frank.[28]

Still, it may be true that of the two parents, Mollie displayed an even greater tendency to pamper Scott. From the time of his infancy and beyond, she showed extreme concern for his health, no doubt afraid that he would become the third child in the family to die young. In his ledger, Fitzgerald writes be-

side the margin for June 1899 that his mother "feared con-
sumption" when he developed a "persistent cough." The ledger
includes other examples of his mother's overprotectiveness.
Throughout his childhood, she would urge him to lie down or
take warm baths, and in cold weather, she bundled him in multiple layers of clothing. Time was running out for her to raise a
child who would live past infancy, since she was already in her
late thirties when he was born. In January 1900 came further
reason to become anxious about him. Fitzgerald recounts in his
ledger, "His mother presented him with a sister who lived only
an hour."[29] And he writes of two more difficult moments in the
next month in his life: he caught measles and also swallowed a
penny. Not surprisingly, then, when he began nursery school
the next month and began to bawl, his parents postponed his
education after just one day. He was in his third year at the
time, the age at which Louise had died.

Instead of working through their grief, both parents seem to
have kept it alive. After Louise Scott and Mary Ashton's
deaths, Edward wrote to his mother, "I wonder sometimes if I
will ever have any interest in life again, perhaps so but certainly the keen zest of enjoyment is gone forever."[30] Indeed, he
demonstrated little keen zest for the rest of his life, acting le-
thargically and drinking "too much," as Scott would write in
his ledger. Several financial losses—he experienced professional difficulty before and after his daughters' deaths—would
have further intensified his grief. Likely drawing upon his impression of his father, Fitzgerald refers to Amory's father in
This Side of Paradise (1920) as "unassertive" and "lifeless,"
words that would also describe Gatsby's father in *The Great
Gatsby* (1925).

Mollie also demonstrated symptoms of chronic, underlying
grief. As Turnbull states, she "buried her grief," never speaking of the daughters' deaths in later years.[31] The repression, at
least in a public sense, appears to have begun immediately
after the deaths. Mary's obituary in the *St. Paul Pioneer Press*
notes "funeral private." If Louise was sick at this time—it was
less than seven months before her death—Edward and Mollie
may have wished for her sake to avoid a large outpouring of
sadness. In July 1901, when Mollie was in her forties, she gave
birth to Annabel, a daughter who would live past infancy, but

she remained a highly anxious person, as if continually under the influence of turbulent, partially repressed emotions. Fitzgerald once described her as "half insane with pathological nervous worry" (LFSF, 199). Once, she could not help from blurting out to a friend whose husband was terminally ill, "I'm trying to decide how you'll look in mourning." Since she generally wore black crape dresses, Mollie could identify with a woman in mourning wear. Though she threw out Fitzgerald's juvenilia, she held onto Louise's dolls throughout her life. The dolls resemble linking objects, items that encourage the externalization of grief. She kept them out of sight, wrapping them in tissue paper. In a scrapbook she kept of her son's accomplishments, she had demonstrated her unresolved mourning, her desire for reunion with her daughters: "Louise and Mary's little brother made his first attempt to walk and it seems as if they were nearer."[32] Here, in a rare reference to her daughters, Fitzgerald is not mentioned by name. But he has temporarily rescued his mother from her grief.

Fitzgerald suggests in his largely autobiographical sketch "An Author's Mother" that throughout his mother's life, her daughters seemed as alive to her as he did. For the sketch, he invents a situation in which a senile woman, dressed in black crape, visits a department store to purchase a birthday present for her son Hamilton. However, she becomes sidetracked by thoughts of his "peculiar" career as an author, and further sidetracked by her desire to purchase a book of poetry that she prefers to his writing. Then she falls down, injures her head, and is brought to a hospital. Believing she has been brought to her home, she says, "Don't disturb my son John or my son-in-law or *my daughter that died* or my son Hamilton who—" (emphasis mine).[33] Before thinking of her son Hamilton, she recalls her deceased daughter. And she pauses after she does think of him, struggling to remember who he is and what he does in life. Fitzgerald has the mother die from her head injury at the end of this sketch, though Mollie was alive at the time he wrote it. The emotionally distant fathers in Fitzgerald's first two novels are also killed off, much to the author's father's displeasure.

However, like a living linking object struggling to assimilate the mourning parent's grief, Fitzgerald was sometimes able to identify, even consciously empathize, with his parents' sense of loss. His father's mode of mourning and his father's native South were paired in his mind: when he empathized with his father's sense of loss, he thought of the Old South, and when he admired the spirit of the Old South, his thoughts evoked his view of his father's grief. We see this mental association in a 1940 letter he wrote to his Cousin after his father and her mother had died: "I wonder how deep the Civil War was in them. . . . How lost they seemed in the changing world" (LFSF, 419–20). And we see this association in reverse in a letter to Laura Guthrie in 1935 about his experiences in Baltimore:

> I love it more than I thought—it is so rich with memories—it is nice to look up the street and see the statue of my great [paternal] uncle and to know Poe is buried here and that many ancestors of mine have walked in the old town by the bay. I belong here, where everything is civilized and gay and rotted and polite. (LFSF, 531)

Demonstrating his uncommon sense of generational continuity and history as a whole, he suggests that southerners of today and yesterday, including his ancestors, share an ability to remain "gay" and "polite" amidst their "rotted," vanishing way of life. He words recall his belief that his father once demonstrated a similar grace under the pressure of loss. Fitzgerald writes in "The Death of My Father" that his father was able to take care of him, even though the two eldest sisters had died just months before his birth, and even though his father came from "tired old stock."

Fitzgerald's identification with his father's mode of grief is also recalled in his reference to Poe. Edward was fond of Poe and Byron, poets who dwelled upon the problem of loss, and Fitzgerald was quick to recall that when he was a boy, his father had read these poets aloud to him. In a letter to his mother dated June 1930, Fitzgerald writes of his visit to the place in Switzerland that inspired Byron's "The Prisoner of Chillon," and he refers as well to Poe: "Tell Father I visited the '—seven pillars of Gothic mould / in Chillon's dungeons deep and old' and thought of the first poem I ever heard, or was [it] 'The Raven'?" (LFSF, 495–96) In a letter written shortly afterwards to his mother, he refers to "Father's Castle of Chillon," as if his father lived there. Fitzgerald is nostalgically alluding

to the fact that his father used to read to him a poem in which
a son jailed atop Mount Chillon mourns for his deceased brothers and father, ultimately transcending his sense of grief and
confinement—more grace under pressure—by tapping into the
romantic world of his imagination. And Fitzgerald also recalls
as an adult that his father read him Poe's poem of a "weak and
weary" man who cannot overcome his grief. We can understand why both poems would carry enormous emotional reso-
nance for both father and son. Readers of Fitzgerald's fiction
readily observe its often romantic attitude toward loss.

Fitzgerald was also able to identify with his mother's mode
of mourning, albeit with greater difficulty. In a 1936 letter to
his sister, he described his experience of sorting through their
mother's possessions after she was taken from her residence,
suffering from an illness that would soon take her life:

> It was sad taking her from the hotel, the only home she knew for
> fifteen years, to die—and to go thru her things. The slippers and
> corset she was married in, Louisa's dolls in tissue paper, old letters
> and souvenirs, and collected scrap paper, and diaries that began
> and got nowhere, all her prides and sorrows and disappointments
> all come to nothing, and her lugged away like so much useless flesh
> the world had got thru with—
>   Mother and I never had anything in common except a relentless
> stubborn quality, but when I saw all this it turned me inside out
> realizing how unhappy her temperament made her and how she
> clung, to the end, to all things that would remind her of moments
> of snatched happiness. So I couldn't bear to throw out anything,
> even that rug, and it all goes to storage. (LFSF, 535)

We cannot state with certainty why Fitzgerald mistakenly refers to Louise as Louisa, as if he believed his sister had the
same name as Mollie's mother Louisa. Possibly his mistake
stems from the fact that the daughters' deaths were not referred to in the family. We can state with certainty, however,
that Fitzgerald provides a glimpse here into his mother's
mourning behavior, her habit of clinging nostalgically to the
dolls and anything else—including himself, we might add—
that reminded her of lost happiness. Accordingly, in "An Author's Mother," he depicts the mother as an admirer of
nostalgic, sentimental poets such as Longfellow and the Cary

sisters, Alice and Phoebe. The Cary sisters wrote scores of poems in which people who met an early demise are idealized. Significantly, though, he describes his mother as "stubborn" in the letter to his sister, revealing his pejorative attitude toward her grief; he also admits that he has the same stubborn quality. He demonstrates her retentiveness and repressiveness in moving her possessions into storage, taking none of them home with him, and forming no apparent plan for what to do with them in the future. The Thomas Cooper Library at the University of South Carolina has recently purchased one of Louise's dolls for its Fitzgerald collection. It has frequently been observed that Fitzgerald's fiction, often written in impressive bursts of energy that recall his mother's near-manic nature, sometimes smacks of sentimentality.

Thus, under the threat of maternal loss, Fitzgerald identifies with her grief, much as he identified with his father's grief after his father's death. The living linking object, we recall, avoids object loss in childhood by assuming the parents' bereaved manner. Both parents' modes of mourning, as perceived through Fitzgerald's eyes, were reflected in his everyday thoughts and his creative work.

Mourning and Melancholia

Throughout his life, Fitzgerald suffered from a proneness toward depression. Comparing himself with Hemingway, he once wrote, "His inclination is toward megalomania and mine toward melancholy" (LFSF, 543). Fitzgerald came to think of unhappiness as normal, as he indicates in a question he once posed in a letter to the young Turnbull: "what do you care about happiness—and who does except the perpetual children of this world?" (LFSF, 505). We might question whether Fitzgerald's inclination toward melancholia accords with the conventional portrait of him as the son of doting parents. His claim that they spoiled him—that they were, in fact, overprotective—may conceal the sense that they were underprotective. It is worth noting that we repeatedly see doting mothers in his fiction, such as Beatrice and Daisy in *This Side of Paradise* and

The Great Gatsby respectively, who seem distanced, if not estranged, from their children.

Fitzgerald's views on parenthood have likely encouraged the misleading biographical accounts. He made sweeping generalizations about child-rearing, taking his place among various intellectuals in the early twentieth century, such as John B. Watson, the founder of behaviorism, whom Fitzgerald admired. Watson sought to destroy the Victorian exaltation of motherhood, participating in the "matricidal" nature of modern American culture.[34] Fitzgerald may not have read Watson's writings, but he would have known about his ideas, since Watson's reputation in early-twentieth-century America even outrivaled Freud's. As Watson would have wished, Fitzgerald attempted to raise his daughter to become "tough as nails," as if he wished to avoid duplicating his parents' behavior. His fiction often provides warnings against loving a child "too much"—such as at the end of *This Side of Paradise* and in "Babylon Revisited" (1930). His view is contradicted by psychoanalysis, which has found that those who receive inadequate parenting are particularly prone to depressive disorders.[35] We can readily see how Fitzgerald might have developed a proneness toward depression after growing up among parents who unsuccessfully attempt to mask their preoccupation with their daughters by idealizing him.

THE FAMILY PARVENU

The child of secretly preoccupied parents becomes an outsider in the family. Biographers have frequently referred to Fitzgerald's sense of otherness, attributing it to his youth among multitudes of wealthier non-Catholics in St. Paul, at prep school, and at Princeton. Indeed, he attributed his "two-cylinder inferiority complex" to the fact that he was "half black Irish [on his mother's side] and half old American stock [on his father's]" (LFSF, 503). He made this admission after his friend John O'Hara expressed admiration for the depiction of the parvenu Lew Lowrie in "More Than Just a House" (1933). In the context of the present study, it is noteworthy that Lew gains social prestige not only by accruing wealth but also by saving the lives of two sisters. The sisters come from an old-money family, and their mother—a woman consumed with thoughts of the past, as is her husband—feels so appreciative of his rescue that she invites him into the family's social circle.

Given his role as familial outsider, it makes sense that he identified with the underdog from a very early age. He writes autobiographically in "The Romantic Egotist," his unpublished first novel, about a story his protagonist had read as a child:

> First there was a book that was I think *one of the big sensations of my life.* It was nothing but a nursery book, but it filled me with the saddest and most yearning emotion. I have never been able to trace it since. It was about a fight that the large animals, like the elephant, had with the small animals, like the fox. The small animals won the first battle; but the elephants and lions and tigers finally overcame them. The author was prejudiced in favor of the large animals, but my sentiment was all with the small ones. I wonder if even then I had a sense of the wearing-down power of big, respectable people. *I can almost weep now* when I think of that poor fox, the leader—the fox has somehow typified the innocence to me ever since.[36] (emphasis mine)

The story initially made such an enormous impact that the adult protagonist (Fitzgerald) still feels a desire to cry in thinking of the smaller animals' plight. It is doubtful that a child reading simple nursery books like this could have already developed such a profound identification with the underdog from an appreciation of society's ethnic and economic stratification.

When he enrolled in the St. Paul Academy in 1908, Fitzgerald acted like an outsider from the beginning, continually boasting in order to gain others' admiration, but gaining their derision instead. He wrote a story entitled "Reade, Substitute Right Half," in which a small boy earns heroic status after coming off the bench and starring in a football game. A few years before he had written this story, he had developed another fantasy of substituting for another. As he writes in his ledger beside the margin for January 1905, "Suspicious he is a changeling."[37] He explains this fantasy in "An Author's House," also noting that he felt a need to "bury" it, as if out of shame: "I buried my first childish love of myself, my belief . . .

that I wasn't the son of my parents but a son of a king, a king who ruled the whole world."[38] Significantly, Fitzgerald is admitting to his grandiosity just a few sentences after referring to his sisters' deaths. Drawing upon Freud's discussion of the "family romance," we can posit a connection between Fitzgerald's belief in his royal lineage and his relationship with parents preoccupied with their deceased daughters. Freud found that when children feel "dissatisfied" with their parents and compare them with those of other children, they often come to believe they are the children of more esteemed parents, especially nobly born ones. This part of Freudian theory accords with Fitzgerald's resentment of his flighty, unattractive mother and his lethargic father. One writer has cited the Freudian theory in discussing Fitzgerald's fantasy, and many biographers, without citing Freud, have intuited that Fitzgerald's fantasy indicates his feelings of superiority toward his parents.[39] However, there is more to Freud's theory that bears relevance here. Freud explains that the child's feeling of dissatisfaction with the parents arises from an earlier feeling of being "slighted." In other words, the child's sense of superiority conceals a sense of inferiority. Freud elaborates: "There are only too many occasions on which a child is slighted, or at least *feels* he has been slighted, on which he feels he is not receiving the whole of his parents' love, and, most of all, on which he feels regrets at having to share it with brothers and sisters"— usually older ones.[40]

Freud's theory of the family romance provides a new perspective on the parvenu theme in Fitzgerald's fiction. While the protagonists of his four completed novels suffer from an extraordinary desire to be accepted by others, to receive their love and support, only one of those heroes, Jimmy Gatz / Jay Gatsby, is convincing as an economic and ethnic outsider. The protagonists in *This Side of Paradise* and *The Beautiful and Damned* (1922), Amory Blaine and Anthony Patch respectively, become poor only when they are adults, and desperately crave others' affections before then. In *Tender Is the Night*, Dick Diver grows up in modest circumstances, yet a consideration of his socioeconomic concerns yields only a limited explanation of his intense desire to be loved by Nicole and everyone else he meets. One characteristic these three protagonists, as well as Gatsby, have in common is that they all seek the love of people, such as Beatrice, Daisy, Nicole, and Grandfather Patch in *The Beautiful and Damned*, who display a marked preoccupation with some loss in their pasts. I will take up this issue at length in subsequent chapters.

EPIC GRANDEUR OR GRANDIOSITY?

Fitzgerald once told Laura Guthrie: "I don't know why I can write stories. I don't know what it is in me or that comes to me when I start to write. I am half feminine—at least my mind is."[41] Since he also attributed his creativity to the deaths of his sisters, we might look for a connection between his "half feminine" nature and his role as a living linking object. Possibly his identification with his sisters included an identification with their perceived gender traits. Certainly Fitzgerald was aware that the deceased can contribute to a child's sense of gender, for in *Tender Is the Night*, Rosemary has been raised to take on the "hard" ("masculine") traits of her deceased father and stepfather. Accordingly, she develops the ability to flirt with her director and have affairs with numerous men without becoming bogged down in "feminine" emotion.

Given the limitation of biographical evidence here, we should examine the connection between Fitzgerald's sisters' deaths and his sense of gender in another, more certain light. In sharing his parents' modes of grief, Fitzgerald demonstrated behavior that he, sharing a common cultural view, considered feminine. He expresses this belief in an August 1935 letter to H. L. Mencken after Mencken's wife died:

> I suppose like most people whose stuff is creative fiction there is a touch of the feminine in me (never in *any* sense *tactile*—I have always been woman crazy, God knows)—but there are times when it is nice to think that there are other wheel horses pulling the whole load of human grief + dispair, + trying to the best of their ability to mould it into form—the thing that made Lincoln sit down in Jeff Davis' chair in Richmond and ask the guards to leave him alone there for a minute.[42]

Here Fitzgerald again associates femininity with creativity, and he further associates it with the willingness to confront loss. He admits to curiosity over Mencken's effort, as a male, to accept grief and despair. And he thinks as well of two other males experiencing loss—Lincoln, pausing to empathize with Jefferson Davis. The Lincoln reference recalls Fitzgerald's admiration, expressed in a prior letter to Gerald and Sara Murphy, of the president's eloquent words of condolence for a woman who had lost four sons in the war (LFSF, 426), words recently made especially well-known through the movie *Saving Private Ryan*. In his letter to Mencken, Fitzgerald admits, after cautioning Mencken not to consider him a homosexual, that he shares the "feminine" willingness to assume the burden of grief. He was experiencing grief over Zelda's institutionalization for her schizophrenia at the time.

Fitzgerald traces that willingness back to his childhood in "The Death of My Father." There, one sentence before he refers to his father's attempt to take care of him in the aftermath of his sisters' deaths, he writes, "I loved my father—always deep in my subconscious I have referred judgments back to him, what he would have thought or done."[43] Thus, from his childhood and beyond, he identified with his father's efforts to carry the load of family tragedy. Since Fitzgerald had the capacity to make his sisters "seem nearer" just by attempting to walk, to rescue his mother (and father?) at least momentarily from the pain of mourning, we can understand his deep-seated identification with his father's grief. Before he looked to Mencken and Lincoln, he looked to his father for an example of how to integrate his role as a linking object, as a "mourning savior," with those "masculine" traits uniquely his own.

Throughout his life, he demonstrated a deeply divided nature—to empathize with others or to withdraw from them in search of self-reliance. We see this dichotomy in the "crack-up" essays. Attempting to explain his "crack-up," he writes of his consuming efforts to help others. He states, for example, "I saw honest men through moods of suicidal gloom."[44] He empathized with others so vividly that he came to fear he had permanently merged egos with them: *I had become identified with the objects of my horror or compassion.*[45] His self-diagnosis thus resembles his view of Ring Lardner, expressed in another essay. In the memorial essay "Ring," Fitzgerald recalls his friend's "cosmic sense of responsibility": the "woes of many people haunted him . . . it was as if he believed he could and ought to do something about such things."[46] Fitzgerald eventually chose to shirk his own cosmic sense of responsibility. In the final essay, he decides that he will "cease any attempts to be a person—to be kind, just, or generous."[47]

There were in fact many times in Fitzgerald's life, including before his crack-up, when he was unkind, unjust, and ungenerous, as if he were withdrawing in a narcissistic rage. Sara Murphy once wrote to him, "I have always told you you haven't the faintest idea what anybody else but yourself is like."[48] However, even after his crack-up, Fitzgerald often demonstrated an intense compassion for others. Sometimes his compassion bordered on grandiosity, but when tamed, his desire to empathize served a positive function. Turnbull recalls that Fitzgerald "had the knack of breaking down your defenses, of making you feel there was nothing you couldn't say to him, just as he was quick to open up his own life to you."[49] Sheilah Graham describes his "gift of making you believe you are the most thoughtful, perceptive person."[50] Fitzgerald helped to educate Graham in literature, a role he also attempted to perform for his daughter and numerous writers less accomplished than he. The writer Rebecca West was highly impressed by an occasion in 1930 when she watched Emily Vanderbilt telling him of her troubles. Vanderbilt's distress was probably severe at the time—she would one day commit suicide—but Fitzgerald was helpful. He was "showing this wonderful gentleness and charity which I remember as his great characteristic."[51]

Despite his often cynical attitude toward his parents, he felt a desire to help them. After his father lost his salesman's job in Buffalo in 1908, Fitzgerald returned the quarter his mother had given him. Later, she told him to go speak to his father and, as if born for the role, he went over to him and attempted to make him feel important, asking him if Taft would become the next president. Later in his life, his cousin Cecilia served as a surrogate grieving parent for him to rescue. In *This Side of Paradise*, Fitzgerald writes of Amory's extreme compassion for Clara, a character modeled after Cecilia. In the novel, Amory finds it so disturbing that Clara is coping with her widowhood and motherhood on her own that his overwhelming urge to take care of her cannot be sated.

As a young man, Fitzgerald came to empathize with an older man, Monsignor Fay, believing that the priest suffered from a feeling of loss. After learning of Fay's death, Fitzgerald wrote in a 1919 letter to Shane Leslie, "I think he wanted to die. Deep under it all he had a fear of that blending of the two worlds [Victorian and modern?], that sudden change of values that sometimes happened to him and put a vague unhappiness into the stray corners of his life" (LFSF, 374). We might see the learned, attractive cousin Cecilia and the learned Monsignor Fay as the exalted "parents" in Fitzgerald's family romance. To Fitzgerald, these new "parents" retained the real parents' grief, and that quality intrigued him.

Interestingly, Fitzgerald felt a desire to "replace" Fay. He wrote in a subsequent letter to Leslie, "This [Fay's death] has made me nearly sure I will become a priest. I feel as if in a way his mantle had descended upon me—a desire, or more, to some day recreate the atmosphere of him" (LFSF, 375). Meyers describes this statement as "heartfelt insincerity," yet given the circumstances surrounding Fitzgerald's birth, it is understandable that he suddenly felt a compulsion to "recreate" Fay and only later retreated from his grandiose desire.[52] He did in fact feel at the time that Fay had "descended upon" him, for he thought he had seen Fay's ghost on the day of his death. Raised in a "haunted" environment, it is not surprising that he had developed a belief in ghosts as a child. According to his ledger, a girl told him a ghost story when he was ten that had "scared him silly."

His attraction to Zelda also appears to have been strengthened by her strong interest in loss. Like Fitzgerald and his mother, Zelda demonstrated a tenacious vitality that masked a darker nature. One night when Zelda suddenly decided she wished to see a corpse, she and Fitzgerald spent an uncanny night at a morgue in New York City.[53] Fitzgerald had written "The Ice Palace" (1920) after walking through a graveyard with Zelda in her hometown of Montgomery, Alabama. He explained once, "She told me I could never understand how she felt about the Confederate graves, and I told her I understood so well that I could put it on paper."[54] Apparently he partially took her to mean that he, as a male, could not appreciate the importance of mourning. In the story, Sally Carrol Happer's boyfriend struggles to understand her attraction to a local cemetery. He struggles because he is a northerner, and northerners in the story are "canine"—a code word Sally Carrol uses to describe "masculine" behavior in either sex. Here the connection between southernness and grief evokes Fitzgerald's identification with his father's sense of loss.

Zelda's childhood appears to have fostered her strong interest in death and dying. She writes in her largely autobiographical novel *Save Me the Waltz* that the heroine's mother has a "stoic and unalterable optimism," for she confronts "the sorrows of life with the mournfulness of a Greek chorus."[55] A chief sorrow was the loss of her infant son. This event has affected the heroine's father as well, for he is a solemn, distant man who "might have borne a closer relationship to his family had he not lost his only boy in infancy."[56] Zelda writes here of circumstances that followed her sibling's death before her birth. Like the fictional father, Mr. Sayre was an emotionally distant man, and like the fictional mother, Mrs. Sayre attempted to adopt a stoical attitude toward her loss. At first she responded to her son's death by shutting herself away in her bedroom, but when a doctor told her she had to take care of her daughter Marjorie, she returned to the family. She gave birth to two more children, and then when Zelda was born, her final child, she doted upon her, as if finally able to vent her pent-up emotions. She breastfed Zelda until the age of four. In *Save Me the Waltz*, Zelda writes that the protagonist's mother had "a trick of transference that tided her over to the birth of the last child."[57] Zelda's tomboyishness and competitiveness with males becomes especially interesting in light of her parents' unresolved grief for their son.

Fitzgerald, who resented the way his mother had attempted to spoil him in reaction to her grief, always felt that Zelda's psychological troubles in later life related to her upbringing. When he gave Zelda's father a copy of Watson's *Behaviorism*, he may have been taking a backhanded swipe at him for allowing Zelda's mother to pamper her. In *Tender Is the Night*, the schizophrenic Nicole was raised by a father who doted upon her so intensely that he committed incest with her. Despite Fitzgerald's aversion to one aspect of Zelda's upbringing, his understanding of the Sayres' experience with loss also drew him closer to her. He was fascinated by her interest in spiritualism and theosophy, sister religions that attracted people in mourning. The central ritual of spiritualism, the seance, afforded mourners a special opportunity to seek a reunion with deceased loved ones. And theosophy provided an eschatological basis for seances, since it mapped out an extensive vision of the afterworld combining astrology, Hindu reincarnation, and other bodies of thought. In his fiction, Fitzgerald dealt with these occult religions' particular appeal to those in mourning. In *The Beautiful and Damned*, Gloria turns to an esoteric religion after her parents die. Thus, Fitzgerald would have understood the likely origin of Mrs. Sayre's interest in theosophy, which she passed on to Zelda.

Zelda consulted a medium, a Mrs. Francesca, to find out if she should marry Fitzgerald. Zelda tried Mrs. Francesca's ouija board but kept getting the word "dead" again and again—an unsurprising result in light of her inclination toward morbidity. But Mrs. Francesca had better results with the board, for she found out that Zelda and Fitzgerald were "soul-mates," that they should get married. Drawing upon theosophical belief, Zelda attempted to explain the concept of the soul mate in a letter to Fitzgerald. She wrote that "two souls are incarnated together—not necessarily at the same time but are mated—since the time when people were bi-sexual."[58] Kenneth Lynn has written that Fitzgerald "was utterly beguiled by this letter. Scott was Zelda and Zelda was Scott: the more he thought about this idea, the more meanings he discovered in it, as did Zelda."[59] The "half-feminine" Fitzgerald, born after the deaths of female siblings and a believer in ghosts, need not have looked far to see one such meaning in his uncanny prenatal twinhood with a tomboyish young woman. He and Zelda were triumphing over their sense of mortality by envisioning themselves as two souls eternally united.

On a more mundane level, Fitzgerald again demonstrated his sense of kinship with those touched by loss through his concern for the Murphys after their elder son died of spinal meningitis. Fitzgerald wrote to them that when he was undergoing his crack-up, he thought of the fact that they had just lost their son, and he reflected that his own troubles paled in comparison: "I reminded myself that nothing had happened to me with the awful *suddenness* of your tragedy of a year ago, nothing so utterly conclusive and irreparable" (LFSF, 425). When the Murphys' younger son died of tuberculosis less than two years after the death of the elder son, Fitzgerald wrote a January 1937 letter expressing his understanding of the depths of their tragedy and also pointing out their surviving hope in their daughter Honoria:

> Another link binding you to life is broken and with such insensate cruelty that [it] is hard to say which of the two blows was conceived with more malice. . . . But I can see another generation growing up around Honoria and an eventual peace somewhere, an occasional port of call as we all sail deathward. Fate can't have any more arrows in its quiver for you that will wound like these. Who was it said that it was astounding how the deepest griefs can change in time to a sort of joy? The golden bowl [in *Ecclesiastes*] is broken indeed but it *was* golden; nothing can ever take those boys from you now. (LFSF, 426–27)

Their surviving child will carry on the family tradition, he observes, speaking from personal experience.

LIVING WITH THE DECEASED

We recall that according to Freud, the double initially provides a sense of triumph over death, but then a reminder of submission to death. We further recall that living linking objects, who experience a particularly intense "relationship," with their deceased "double," are prone to both a sense of immortality and a phobic nature. A similar contradiction existed in Fitzgerald. When he acknowledges his childhood changeling fantasy in "An Author's House," he also reveals his childhood belief that he "would never die like other people."[60] At the same time, he also demonstrated hypochondria from an early age. His hypochondria was so severe that, even long before his alcoholism had ruined his health, he believed he would die young.[61]

We recall still further that, however much they may or may not fear death, living linking objects are prone to self-destructiveness. Inward-directed rage and low self-esteem, arising from the competition with the double, encourage this self-destructiveness. Fitzgerald demonstrated an attraction to death throughout his life. His night spent at the morgue and his enjoyment in viewing a book of photographs showing soldiers with their heads blown off demonstrate a streak of morbidity. Moreover, he suffered from numerous illnesses, squandered his vast earnings, became an alcoholic, experienced recurrent suicidal ideation, attempted suicide in 1936 after he was derisively portrayed in *The New York Post*, and ultimately met an early death in 1940. While each separate problem can be attributed to multiple causes, all of them taken together suggest an underlying self-destructiveness.

At the same time, however, a relationship with a "double" can prove beneficial, as Fitzgerald's dictum would suggest: "There never was a good biography of a good novelist. There couldn't be. He is too many people if he's any good."[62] As a male willing to confront the problem of loss—*This Side of Paradise*, *The Great Gatsby*, and *Tender Is the Night* all include pivotal graveyard scenes, and *The Last Tycoon* was to end with a funeral—Fitzgerald displayed one way in which a writer might take on such a composite personality.

2

The Short Stories: Mourning
Becomes Electra?

In 1931, FITZGERALD WROTE OUT A TRANSCRIPT OF A DREAM HE HAD experienced that intrigued him. He gave the transcript to his friend Margaret Turnbull, a participant in a Jung discussion group. Her son Andrew prints the complete transcript in his biography. The dream begins with Fitzgerald in an upstairs apartment with his mother, whom he notes is "clumsy and in mourning, as she is today."[1] Indeed, Edward Fitzgerald had recently died. The image of his mother in mourning also appears to relate to a past situation in Fitzgerald's life, for as the dream proceeds, Fitzgerald walks into another room where he encounters a group of "handsome and rich" men whom he feels he knew "slightly as a child." They act snobbishly toward him—perhaps, Fitzgerald notes in his transcript, because he is not wealthy and socially respected—and he learns that he has not been invited to a dance downstairs. He feels that he would have been invited if the men appreciated "how important" he was. Later, he views the preparations for the dance and runs into one of the snobbish young men, whereupon he "loses all poise and stammers something absurd."[2] He leaves the house, and his mother calls out to him. However, he becomes disgusted by her—possibly, Fitzgerald notes in the transcript, because she is "clinging" to him, because she shows "pity" for him, and because she is socially awkward—and he makes a "terse and furious" comment to her.

His mother does not appear in the rest of the dream. The manifest content of this part of the dream, as Turnbull notes, reflects Fitzgerald's "embarrassment over his mother."[3] Interestingly, in the dream, Fitzgerald's embarrassment and resentment arise after he comes into contact with a mother who is silent and in mourning. And when she does speak to him, perhaps "clinging" to him, he reacts bitterly. This situation strongly recalls Fitzgerald's childhood, in which his mother, preoccupied with his sisters, eventually clung to him yet remained preoccupied with loss. Accordingly, though Fitzgerald's critics and biographers have not pointed out the similarity between his dream and "Crazy Sunday"—the story was written in January 1932 while the dream occurred after his father's death in 1931—the story hinges upon a recent mother's mourning behavior. Like the dream, "Crazy Sunday" features an early scene involving a young man and a mother; portrays the young man's loneliness and embarrassment; and then describes the woman's attempt to comfort him out of pity. When she clings to him at the end of the story after her husband's death, he thinks of her as a "little gamin," much as Fitzgerald responds with a "terse and furious reproach" to his grieving mother in the dream.

In several other stories, Fitzgerald depicts mothers unable to work through the process of mourning, alternately distanced from and clinging to the world around them. In this chapter, beginning with an analysis of "Crazy Sunday," I will examine the theme of the mourning mother in Fitzgerald's stories, illuminating their portrayal of female characters.

CAPTIOUSNESS AND HOSTILITY

The theme of mourning in "Crazy Sunday" provides the serious element in a seriocomic story. The comic element comes from the commonplace oedipal content of the story. The protagonist, Joel Coles, learns of the "mother complex" of Miles Calman, a prominent Hollywood director. Calman has learned from his psychoanalyst that his unsatisfying sexual relations with his wife, Stella, stem from the fact that he has "transferred his mother complex" to her, satisfying his libido only in adulterous relationships.[4] Were "Crazy Sunday" to focus seriously on such a prototypical "mother complex," it would feature a trite storyline. But Fitzgerald treats this theme farcically by elaborating on it blatantly and repetitiously. Joel has a "mother complex" too, for he flatters both Stella and Miles's mother, likely seeking to gain their support. The story ends with a final, decisive indication of Joel's fixation on Stella. Having become involved in a romantic relationship with her, he realizes that he cannot end it.

Fitzgerald complicates the story, and also darkens its import, by interweaving the issue of mourning with the "mother complex" issue. Near the beginning of the story, as soon as Joel arrives at the Calman's party and meets Stella, he fears that she is preoccupied with loss. Accordingly, we have learned in the story's opening that Joel was raised by a preoccupied mother. Because of his mother's itinerant acting career, he "spent his childhood between London and New York trying to separate the real from the unreal." (SFSF, 403). We are thus led to suspect that his mother was itinerant not only professionally, but also maternally—that her love for him was intermittent and inadequate while she was distracted by her career. Now he attempts to win over Stella, who is also an actress, saying to her:

> "So you have a baby? . . . That's the time to look out. After a pretty woman has had her first child, she's very vulnerable, because she wants to be reassured about her own charm. She's got to have some new man's unqualified devotion to prove to herself she hasn't lost anything." (SFSF, 404)

Joel fears that she is preoccupied with a sense of loss surrounding her new motherhood.[5] In showing Stella his sympathy, he likely wishes to make sure that she is not distracted from him. His attitude toward her parallels his feelings toward all the Hollywood bigwigs in attendance at the party. He feels lonely and out of place, and in order to gain their attention, he performs a skit before everyone present. However, his skit does not go over well, for the audience disapproves of his parody of a Hollywood producer. He may well have wished in part to offend the very people whom he has attempted to entertain, as if to revenge himself on them for allowing him to feel lonely.

Though he has met "the thumbs-down of the *clan*" (SFSF, 407; emphasis mine), Stella is one family member, as it were, who has shown him her unconditional love, gazing upon him throughout his performance with her "radiant, never faltering smile" (SFSF, 406). When Joel writes to Miles and Stella in order to express his apology for the sketch the next day, she continues to show support (pity?), telling him by telegram that he was a valued member of the party. She and Joel become closer and closer to each other, but he still fears that she is secretly concerned with another matter. Now he suspects she is using him as a "pawn" in her battle with her unfaithful husband. When she attempts to express to him her feelings about Miles's neglect and adultery, he only pretends to care, for he does "not quite believe in picture actresses' grief. They have other preoccupations" (SFSF, 410). He feels she harbors an inner coldness toward him, for he is startled to see her "dress like ice-water, made in a thousand pale-blue pieces, with icicles trickling at the throat" (SFSF, 413), and he does not answer her when she asks him if he likes the dress. Still, they eventually make love, learning the next morning of Miles's death in a plane crash. The interior monologue reveals his surprisingly bitter response to her attempts to cling to him for support:

> In her dark groping Stella was trying to keep Miles alive by sustaining a situation in which he had figured—as if Miles' mind could not die so long as the possibilities that had worried him still existed. It was a distraught and tortured effort to stave off the realization that he was dead. (SFSF, 417)

Once again, he fears she is distracted by another matter.

One critic has suggested that the hostile attitude toward the female character in the story's ending reflects only the view of a protagonist whose perceptiveness Fitzgerald has taken pains to undercut throughout the story.[6] Though Fitzgerald does in fact put into question his foolish protagonist's ability to distinguish the "real" from the "unreal," Joel's reaction resembles the ambivalent point of view expressed in two other Fitzgerald stories involving characters in mourning. In "The Last of the Belles" (1929), the unnamed protagonist reacts negatively when he learns of Ailie Calhoun's unresolved mourning for her brother:

> she told me about her brother who had died in his senior year at Yale. She showed me his picture—it was a handsome, earnest face

with a Leyendecker forelock—and told me that when she met
someone who measured up to him she'd marry. I found this family
idealism discouraging; even my brash confidence couldn't compete
with the dead. (SFSF, 242)

Her grief serves as an aspect of her nostalgic yearning to recap-
ture her family's aristocratic past. It is similar to Tom Buchanan's grief for a "more white" civilization in *The Great Gatsby*.
Like Ailie Calhoun and Stella Walker, Charlie Wales in "Babylon Revisited" compares the living with the dead. In that story,
Charlie feels guilt over the death of his wife. As Jeffrey Berman
has written, the "past returns to haunt" Charlie, for "the erotic
dialogue between father and daughter is unmistakably incestuous; they are lovers in word if not deed."[7] As Berman notes,
Charlie is partially aware of his warped desire, for he has already reflected:

The present was the thing—work to do and someone to love. But
not to love too much, for he knew the injury that a father can do
to a daughter or a mother to a son by attaching them too closely:
afterward, out in the world, the child would seek in the marriage
partner the same blind tenderness and, failing probably to find it,
turn against love and life. (SFSF, 397)

Despite his concern about relations between a parent and child
of the opposite sex, Charlie's attitude toward his daughter reveals his wish, fueled by both guilt and nostalgia, to deny his
wife's absence in envisioning Honoria as his dead wife—one of
many signs in the story indicative of the pastness of the present, the difficulty of working through the process of mourning.
Given the attitudes expressed toward mourners in "The Last
of the Belles" and "Babylon Revisited," as well as Fitzgerald's
attitude toward his mother in his dream, we can infer that
Fitzgerald identified very strongly with his protagonist in
"Crazy Sunday." Most likely, we are supposed to believe Joel
is acting reasonably when he refuses to sympathize with Stella.
    Fitzgerald has thus interwoven an ominous element into the
lighthearted oedipal theme of the story. Fitzgerald alludes to
the popular appetite for lighthearted Freudianism in *Tender Is*

the Night, where audiences find the oedipal theme in Rosemary Hoyt's "B" movie *Daddy's Girl* to be both tender and provocative. In writing the alternately tender and bitter "Crazy Sunday," Fitzgerald takes after Miles, his character in the story. As a movie director, Miles attained popularity among a public that wishes "only to be entertained" (SFSF, 406), but he managed to remain the "only American-born director with both an interesting temperament and an artistic conscience" (SFSF, 416). Fitzgerald also takes after Eugene O'Neill—whose work Joel has adapted for the screen—since the playwright dealt with Freudian themes in unusual ways. At the same time, the darkness of Fitzgerald's story, its mother-blaming and also its anti-Semitism,[8] resembles his protagonist's theatrical skit, Joel's "accidental" offending of his spectators.

Fitzgerald had provided another unsympathetic perspective on a mourning mother in a previous story. The message of "The Adjuster" (1925) seems aimed not only at his wife, who had recently given birth to Scottie, but also at his mother. It focuses on Luella Hemple, the young, bored wife of a rich man. She confesses to her friend that she finds little fulfillment in life, that she does not enjoy her responsibilities as housewife and mother. Grieving for the loss of her youthful freedom, she takes minimal interest in her two-year-old son Chuck, and she detests the responsibility of purchasing food and cooking meals. By idealizing Chuck, she conceals her lack of concern for him, as we see when the governess tells her about Chuck's "long walk" in Central Park. Since the boy has just "crawled" over to Luella, it is remarkable that he has walked through the park, but Luella fails to appreciate his accomplishment. She provides a stock response, sounding like Daisy Buchanan: "Well, aren't you a smart boy!"[9] She does not demonstrate concern for her son's health when she learns that he walked into a fountain during his visit to the park, even though, as we soon learn, the April weather is cool enough for her husband to use the fireplace at dusk. She does care for her son, but only, as Christiane Johnson has noted, because he provides her with "narcissistic satisfaction."[10] She delights in the fact that he looks like her.

As if to express resentment toward his icy wife, Charles Hemple has a nervous breakdown, throwing food from the icebox. As he rests in bed to recuperate, Luella is unable to follow through on her plans to separate from him, for she is now forced to become a mother to him too. At the same time, probably as a result of the fountain incident, young Chuck catches the flu. Luella does not change her attitude significantly, for as she checks the warmth of her son's cheek, she pauses to engage in idealization once again, reflecting that he looks like a cherub. And she continues to resist her role as food provider. She wastes time by arguing with the cook, firing her, and then getting into an argument with the employment agency about a new cook. In addition, she asks the nurse to prepare food for Chuck.

Fitzgerald punishes her, for Chuck dies suddenly. She responds by thinking of herself, rather than thinking of the child's tragic fate: "What will become of me now?"[11] As she reflects that Chuck's brush and comb still rest on the bureau in his room, she feels that her son cannot be dead. She is counseled at this time by a Dr. Moon, who first appeared in the story just before the husband's breakdown. Dr. Moon is a doctor only in an abstract sense; his advice throughout the story leads her to accept change, the passage of time. In fact, he is an allegorical character representing time itself, as he suggests at the end of the story when he says, "I am five years."[12] After her encounters with him, she combats both her initial self-absorption and her preoccupation with grief over her son, devoting herself instead to her husband, her new "child." Ultimately, Charles recovers from his breakdown. Then she redirects her attention once again, for in the last paragraph of the story, we learn that she has borne two more children.

Addressing the question of whether this is a socially conservative story, Johnson has noted that "in Fitzgerald's day, the growing woman did not have much of a choice" about her role in life. Johnson further observes that Fitzgerald "does not want to have [Luella] become a perfect housewife; he wants her to become a better person."[13] Though these are important points, a focus on the issue of mourning leads us to a different conclusion about Fitzgerald's portrayal of his female protagonist. Significantly, Fitzgerald does not concern himself with his female character's emotions in the interim between her denial of loss and her acceptance of responsibility, nor does he allow us an opportunity to appreciate her previous sense of loss surrounding her marriage.[14] While Luella supposedly recovers from her losses, Dr. Moon's complete lack of sympathy for her grief would probably only aggravate her sense of social confinement. Curiously, Fitzgerald portrays Luella in a negative light by having her make bland remarks about her son in the beginning of the story, yet Dr. Moon's sententious advice for her—"The more you try to run away from yourself," he says at one point, sounding like Dr. Diver in *Tender Is the Night*, "the more you'll have yourself with you"—does not disqualify him as the story's moral center.[15] True, it makes sense that Dr. Moon, as an abstraction rather than a person, would fail to empathize with Luella—he does not work in the "anthropomorphic business," as Ginzburg, the character representing death in Bernard Malamud's "Idiots First," says of himself. Yet we are given the opportunity to appreciate the protagonist's distress in "Idiots First," while we are distanced from Luella's grief in Fitzgerald's story.

Two Different Views

Unlike "Crazy Sunday" and "The Adjuster," "Family in the Wind" (1932) represents an attempt, albeit a reluctant one, to seek reconciliation with the mourning mother. In the diffuse, and consequently contrived, plot of this story, Dr. Forrest Janney, an alcoholic who no longer practices medicine (qualities reminiscent of Fitzgerald's downward-spiraling life) grieves over the death of a woman. His concern for this much younger woman was likely the flip side of his sense of maternal loss, for he is also drawn toward a little girl named Helen, who showers her maternal feelings onto her pet kitten.

His sister-in-law Rose has been anxious about her son Pinky who, as we learn near the beginning of the story, got into a fight and lies unconscious with a bullet in his brain. Forrest will not operate on Pinky, however, no doubt in part because he resents his nephew. Pinky had been married to the young woman Forrest mourns for, and the nephew shares complicity in her death. However, Forrest eventually attempts to help Pinky's anxious mother. When a tornado strikes and turns the countryside into a "land of mourning," Forrest becomes a lifesaver, providing medical help for the injured. At the time, he also encounters Pinky lying unconscious, and he begins to operate on his nephew. Pinky dies during the operation, and Forrest's responsibility remains ambiguous, but when another tornado strikes, Forrest begins to achieve atonement, for he protects Pinky's brother Butch, leading him under a nearby bridge. In "crawling" under a bridge—the word is repeated several times—and saving Butch's life, Forrest might be seen as simultaneously regressing and progressing, entering a maternal enclave while heroically saving a mother from further grief. However, he does not achieve full reparation, for despite his rescue, Rose continues to mourn—as we would expect—for Pinky. Thus, Forrest is not absolved of guilt. He considers consoling her at the end of the story—in contrast to Joel's behavior in "Crazy Sunday" and Dr. Moon's in "The Adjuster"—but he then thinks that it is "no use. He [is] up against the maternal instinct" (SFSF, 434). He shows concern, but he realizes that it is too great a task for him to single-handedly cure her. Instead, he transfers his concern for her onto someone else. At the end of the story, he ceases drinking in order to take care of the little girl Helen—the girl who mothers her kittens—for she was orphaned in the storms. He will help her to cope with loss.

In "The Ice Palace," Fitzgerald similarly provides polarized views of the mother. But significantly, his identification with "feminine" grief in this story leads to a feminist implication. In the story, Sally Carrol Happer frequents the grave of a woman who died young, before Sally Carrol was born. The deceased woman's name is Margery Lee, a name that sounds very close to "Mary Louise," the names of Fitzgerald's sisters, and also sounds like "Annabel Lee," the name of the "child" mourned for in the eponymous poem by Poe, whom we recall was one of Edward Fitzgerald's favorite authors. In reflecting upon Margery Lee, Sally Carrol imagines her to have been the embodiment of the charming Southern belle, someone "born to stand on a wide, pillared porch and welcome folks in" (SFSF, 65). The stones in the same graveyard marking the Confederate dead also evoke strong feelings for Sally Carrol. She tells her fiancé, Harry Bellamy, that the soldiers "died for the most beautiful thing in the world—the dead South" (SFSF, 66). She identifies with Margery Lee and the soldiers to such a profound degree that she feels her personality is linked with them. She feels a desire to have "the old time," the Old South, "live in" her. Accordingly, she charms people, behaving like one of the last of the belles.

In drawing comfort from her deceased "sibling," Sally Carrol recalls Freud's theory in "The Uncanny" that during the stage of primary narcissism, the double represents a triumph over death. Accordingly, her experience in the South evokes a narcissistic maternal enclave. She spends most of her time "hanging round" in her native Tarleton, Georgia, where "the heat [is] never hostile, only comforting, like a great warm nourishing bosom for the infant earth" (SFSF, 64). Her sense of loss, even when painful, provides her with a sense of security: "Even when I cry"—she says in a visit to the cemetery—"I'm happy here, and I get a sort of strength from it" (SFSF, 66). The child identifying with the deceased "sibling," Margery Lee, receives maternal support.

At the same time, Sally Carrol feels that she cannot exist in this enclave forever. Her identification with the past encourages a narcissistic conflict, for she must learn to take on responsibilities, to carry on the struggles of the dead. In the graveyard, she tells her fiancé that "people have these dreams they fasten onto things, and I've always grown up with that dream" (SFSF, 66). And she has previously said to her friend Clark Darrow, "There's two sides to me, you see. There's the sleepy old side you love; an' there's a sort of energy—the feelin' that makes me do wild things" (SFSF, 64).

Accordingly, she feels she must ambitiously seek a new life in the midwestern hometown of her fiancé, Harry. The martial imagery used in the description of her visit to the North— Harry's surname is Bellamy (*Bellum*: Lat., war)—provides the intimation that she will come into conflict, that she will wage a battle for dominance against the North, taking after the Confederate dead with whom she identifies. She finds that in Harry's hometown, children are pushed to leave the home and excel elsewhere before they can again receive maternal love. Harry states, "We're out in the cold as soon as we're old enough to walk" (SFSF 74). Harry contrasts northerners with southerners, who "put quite an emphasis on family" (SFSF, 69). Appropriately, Harry's mother acts icily toward Sally Carrol. Since idealization often masks a diametrically opposed view, it is not surprising that Fitzgerald's idealization of the maternal South has quickly given way to his highly critical perspective on northern motherhood, the region where Sally Carrol's narcissistic conflict comes into focus.

To be sure, Fitzgerald's perspective on the North has a positive side, for Sally Carrol meets famous athletes and prominent business tycoons in the Midwest. Still, midwesterners remain in a state of mild depression, repressing the depths of their sense of maternal loss, whereas characters in the northeastern wasteland depicted in *The Great Gatsby*, tend to deny the reality of loss to an even greater extent. Sally Carrol observes that the people in her fiancé's hometown have a "certain brooding rigidity" (SFSF, 72), and she laments that "all tears freeze up here" (SFSF, 80)! She thinks of these grief-repressing, unempathic people as "canine," her code word for "masculine." Since a part of Sally Carrol leads her to attempt "wild things," she might be willing to accept "masculine" behavior. But she finds little opportunity to engage in "masculine" pursuits in the North, as well as little opportunity to express her "feminine emotionality." She finds that the women in the North are "glorified domestics. Men are the centre of every mixed group" (SFSF, 74). Whereas she carried conversations at home, she is often ignored in the North.

Under these conditions, Sally Carrol becomes self-destructive. Appropriately, she is associated with Bizet's Carmen. After entering the ice palace, she "accidentally" becomes separated from her fiancé and the others. Harry's faulty empathy probably facilitates the separation. She quickly gives up hope of finding her way out of the enormous structure. She has previously been thinking of her death, imagining herself buried beneath layers of snow, and she feels as if she were escaping into paradise as she confronts the imminent danger of freezing to death. A passage in the palace seems "like the green lane between the parted waters of the Red Sea" (SFSF, 79). In her conflicted mind, the ice palace represents not only a place where she can fulfill her will to die, but also a new maternal enclave. As she comes close to passing out, she senses Margery Lee's presence within the ice palace, and her identification again provides her with a sense of security. She feels her face is being caressed by Margery Lee's "warm soft hands."

Ultimately, she is rescued from the palace. Since Fitzgerald's father temporarily surmounted his sense of grief and undertook responsibility for him when he was an infant, alleviating his sense of maternal loss, it is appropriate that Sally Carrol's rescuer, Roger Patton, recalls Fitzgerald's father. As a lover of literature—he is a professor in the field—and as someone who moved to the Midwest as an adult, Patton resembles Edward Fitzgerald in two ways, ways that Scott Fitzgerald always valued. Moreover, the etymology of the name "Patton" (*pater*: Lat., father) as well as Patton's upbringing in Philadelphia, the city of brotherly love, hints at his fatherly nature. And while Fitzgerald appreciated his father's attempt to take care of him in his infancy, to assume a "maternal" role, Sally Carrol refers to Patton as "feline."

In rescuing her from the ice palace, Patton enables her to return to the comfort of the South. The parallels between Fitzgerald's upbringing and Sally Carrol's experiences suggest that Fitzgerald has displaced his sense of maternal and paternal loss, as well as his "identificatory grief" for his sisters, onto a female character, as if sharing his protagonist's belief that mourning is feminine behavior. In displacing his feelings onto a female character, Fitzgerald develops empathy for the predicament of the marginalized person, and he even includes a transformative implication in Sally Carrol's return to the South. We need not see the South only as a "childlike" place, as one critic has suggested, nor need we see Sally Carrol's return merely as a defense, a "psychic self-preservation," as another has suggested.[16] Rather, on a symbolic level, we may see Sally Carrol's return to the South as an entry into the world of art, where both self-preservation and self-growth are possible. Previously, Sally has associated the ice palace with creativity—the "sunny pleasure-dome" of Coleridge's "Kubla Khan"—and now that she is rescued by a literature professor and is able to return home, the South can fulfill the false promise of that icy deathtrap. Here, she can again express herself and carry conversations. The South is linked with creativity in the first sentence of the story, where "sunlight drip[s] over [Sally Carrol's] house like golden paint over an art jar" (SFSF,

61). Fitzgerald suggests that northerners, in contrast, lack imagination. Looking over the library in the home of her fiancé's family, Sally Carrol noticed that northerners are not readers, for the "books looked as if they had been read—some" (SFSF, 69).

Though "The Ice Palace" is yet another story that provides polarized, unrealistic images of motherhood, Sally Carrol is one grieving woman in Fitzgerald's fiction who is not punished when she resists marriage and motherhood, returning to the South without Harry. The story ultimately suggests that those like Sally Carrol who are forced to face restrictive social norms—women and mourners in particular—can find a voice, carry conversations, by turning to creative expression.

3

Repressed Grief and Victorian Progress in *This Side of Paradise*

LATE IN FITZGERALD'S FIRST NOVEL, *THIS SIDE OF PARADISE*, Amory Blaine pauses to reflect upon the course of his life:

> There were days when Amory resented that life had changed from an even progress along a road stretching ever in sight, with the scenery merging and blending, into a succession of quick, unrelated scenes . . . He felt that it would take all time, more than he could ever spare, to glue these strange cumbersome pictures into the scrap book of his life.[1]

This Side of Paradise similarly lacks structure, for it too contains a "succession of unrelated scenes." Amory's awareness that his life lacks "even progress," then, serves as his creator's metafictional admission that he has failed to adhere to the linear form of the bildungsroman. However, it would not have been appropriate for his protagonist to progress in a straightforward direction, for after all, the novel provides a direct critique of the Victorians' blind faith in inevitable progress.

Late in the novel, Amory criticizes the "heirs of progress," various intellectuals whose ideas, he feels, were tainted by their Victorian sensibility. At first glance, Amory's criticism may seem pretentious, for he has thus far demonstrated only a limited interest in his culture. Indeed, critics have suggested that prior events in the novel do not prepare us for Amory's social statements at the end.[2] However, there are hints in the novel that, on a personal level, Amory's resentment of Victorian progress serves as a reaction against his upbringing, an aspect of his life we have been able to see. He appears to be writing about both his society and his own childhood when he composes a couplet while working on a poem: "Victorians, Victorians, who never learned to weep, / Who sowed the bitter harvest that your children go to reap" (TSOP, 142). On one level, Amory is alluding to the bitter harvest of world war that resulted after the Victorians' blind faith in progress subsumed their effort to confront the failures of the past. On a less-apparent level, Amory might well be writing about his mother's inability to confront her emotions. Much as this couplet is scribbled out by Amory as he composes his poem, the existence of his mother's depression is hidden in the text. In reading *This Side of Paradise* for evidence of her mental anguish and Amory's resulting struggle with empathy for her, we can gain insight into the question of whether or not he progresses over the course of the novel.

FITZGERALD'S DOUBLE

Because the depression of Amory's mother is difficult to perceive, it may be helpful to consider the upbringing of Michael Fane, the protagonist in Compton MacKenzie's *Sinister Street*, since after reading MacKenzie's novel, Amory feels a strong bond with Fane. Fitzgerald's strongest admission of his debt to MacKenzie came in a letter he wrote to a woman who, in reviewing the novel, had accused him of borrowing too freely from *Sinister Street*. Fitzgerald defended the originality of his novel but acknowledged, "I was . . . hindered [in writing the novel] by a series of resemblances between my life and that of Michael Fane which, had I been a more conscientious man, might have precluded my ever attempting an autobiographical novel."[3] Both novels contain lengthy accounts of their protagonist's earliest years, and therein lie some of the resemblances. Let me summarize some of the major aspects of Michael Fane's upbringing.

He is raised for the most part by hired help, since his mother spends long periods away from home, while his father, Michael is told as an infant, has died. Though Michael lacks the maturity to appreciate the importance of his father's death, his mother's absence causes him to feel extreme loneliness. Later in life, he feels uncertain about his own identity and begins wishing to know more about his father's background. Eventually, he learns that he is an illegitimate child, that his father, an English nobleman, has in fact died only recently. He realizes that during his mother's absences from the home, she was spending time with his father. He feels great empathy for her, since she has been forced to endure much unhappiness when away from her lover and has been repressing her grief for years when at home.

Fitzgerald could identify with Michael Fane's experience of being raised by a parent secretly preoccupied with grief. Keeping in mind the childhoods of Michael Fane and Fitzgerald, we can remain attentive to elements of Amory's youth that might otherwise remain unapparent. In addition, one more biographical issue unrelated to Michael Fane's life will help us to interpret *This Side of Paradise*. We further recall from chapter one that while Fitzgerald's parents did not speak of their losses, literature appears to have provided a measure of consolation for them. The pervasive theme of loss in sentimental literature read by Mollie Fitzgerald, as well as in romantic literature read by Edward, stood in sharp contrast to the pre-World War I obsession with industrialization and progress.

MATERNAL DEPRIVATION

While Amory appears to be a thoroughly pampered child, his mother's melancholia distances her from him and promotes a coldness in his personality. Amory would be in particular need of her support, for his father spends his nights holed up in his library sleeping or reading Byron, likely attracted to the poet's theme of isolation. But Beatrice is not a stable parent. When she married, she was "a little bit weary, a little bit sad" (TSOP, 12), and even Amory's birth did not lift her spirits, since he was "carried through a *tiresome* season and brought into the world on a spring day in ninety-six" (TSOP, 12; emphasis mine). In later years, she develops an alcoholic condition and is prone to breakdowns. She expresses an attraction to the other side of paradise, hypochondriacally referring to herself as old and frail—a seeming exaggeration of the truth. And, demonstrating her tendency to express occasional bursts of sentimentality, she tells her son, "I feel my life should have drowsed away close to an older, mellower civilization, a land of greens and autumnal browns" (TSOP, 28). She displaces her hypochondria onto her son, insisting that he take warm baths, sleep in each morning, and be served breakfast in bed, lest he strain his nerves.

Generally, however, Beatrice attempts to hide her inner anxiety. With the exception of her occasional bursts of sentimentality, she usually succeeds in constraining her emotions, as do the Victorians in Amory's couplet. She was originally attracted to Darcy partly because she enjoyed their "unsentimental conversations," and words such as "sensible" and "practical" are integral parts of her working vocabulary. Beatrice insists to Bishop Wiston that she does not need his sympathy: "I do not *want* to talk of myself" (TSOP, 14). She demonstrates a similar desire to avoid betraying emotion when Amory tells her that he wishes to go away to boarding school. She urges him to drop the subject, but a week later, after apparently having composed herself, she tells him he may go away to school.

MATERNAL DEPRIVATION AND NARCISSISM

Amory's desire to go to boarding school most likely arises in part from a desire to distance himself from his preoccupied parents. Before he departs, Beatrice begins to tell him about one of her breakdowns but then stops herself and concludes, "I am not understood, Amory—I know that can't express it to you, Amory, but—I am not understood" (TSOP, 27). Indeed, he fails, or refuses, to understand her, for he snickers at her while she tells him of her problems. We never see him pause to reflect upon the cause or causes of his parents' preoccupation. As if Beatrice is conscious of his uncaring attitude toward her, she tells him, "I want to tell you about your heart—you've probably been neglecting your heart—and you don't *know*" (TSOP, 26).

Amory's treatment of his parents exists as part of an overall narcissistic personality. Appropriately, two of the chapter titles in the novel are "The Egotist Considers" and "Narcissus Off Duty." He demonstrates narcissistic grandiosity, a "van-ity" that most likely serves as a defense against a lack of "self-respect." Moreover, he tends to withdraw from others, as if in a narcissistic rage, for he has "a certain coldness and lack of affection, amounting sometimes to cruelty . . . a shifting sense of honor . . . an unholy selfishness" (TSOP, 25). As a result of these traits, he clings to "a sense of people as automatons to his will, a desire to 'pass' as many boys as possible and get to a vague top of the world" (TSOP, 25). His narcissistic defense probably stems from Mr. and Mrs. Blaine's preoccupied nature. Bowlby's work, we recall, sheds light on such a situation—his view that children often respond to maternal loss by clinging to an extreme self-reliance (similar to narcissistic rage), or by becoming compulsive caregivers for others (similar to narcissistic grandiosity), or by demonstrating both forms of behavior. Since Beatrice demonstrates hypochondria when she emerges from her self-absorption, we are further reminded of Bowlby's finding that a connection also exists in many cases between a parent's hypochondria and the development of compulsive caregiving in a child of that parent.[4]

Accordingly, despite his desire to distance himself from his parents, Amory feels a conflicting need to show concern for his alternately preoccupied and hypochondriacal mother. Beatrice looks to her son at times to be her trusted confidante—her parent, in a sense. He is the only one to whom she expresses her emotions in the novel, and she appears to depend upon him for happiness. He understands his role, for although he snickers when she tells him of her breakdown, he ultimately makes an attempt to console her. He puts his arm around her and says, "Poor Beatrice—Poor Beatrice" (TSOP, 27). His words apparently soothe her, for she then asks him for the first time to tell her how he has been while away at school. Though he understands his caretaking role, it is unlikely that he is truly feeling empathy for her, since he uses similar words for his dog, Count Del Monte, after the dog swallows a box of bluing, loses his mind, and runs away: "Poor little Count," he says. "Oh, *poor little Count!*" (TSOP, 23). Amory later decides that his dog was only pretending to be sick, much as he fails to see his mother's emotional difficulties as serious. Since he feels called upon to play the role of Beatrice's understanding parent, the trope of acting that runs throughout the novel is appropriate. In his relationships with women throughout his life, he behaves as if he were playing a convenient role, as in his relationship with Rosalind, entire passages of which are written in play form. He assumes an exhibitionistic self in order to receive love and approval, behavior that recalls his feelings when he visits his mother during a break at boarding school. At that time, he feels "a quick fear lest he ha[s] lost the requisite charm to measure up to her" (TSOP, 26). Her love for him is conditional.

While Amory's upbringing predisposes him toward self-reliance and compulsive caregiving, his friendship with Monsignor Darcy leads him further down those paths. Darcy harbors the belief that the two of them require no external supports in their lives: "With people like us our home is where we are not" (TSOP, 32), he says. And he further states, "No one person in the world is necessary to you or to me" (TSOP, 32). Later Darcy advises him in a letter, "Beware of losing yourself in the personality of another being, man or woman" (TSOP, 204). He also urges Amory to become a "personage," rather than a personality. A personage, to Darcy, is someone whom others look to as a caretaker. The personage "gathers" experiences that will invite admiration from others: "He's a bar on which a thousand things have been hung—glittering things sometimes, . . . but he uses those things with a cold mentality back of them" (TSOP, 101). When Darcy dies, Amory admires the fact that his friend had taken care of the people at the funeral: "All these people grieved because they had to some extent depended upon Monsignor" (TSOP, 245). He suddenly feels "an immense desire to give people a sense of security" (TSOP, 246). Amory's reaction, though fostered by Darcy, appears to have been instilled in him earlier in life.

Of course Amory's appreciation of the role of caregiver comes late in the novel. Throughout his life, though he demonstrates a predisposition toward both self-reliance and caregiving, only the former tendency is evident at first. His desire to be self-reliant partially conceals a fear that he will lose the support of the many women he courts. When a college classmate, Kerry Holiday, describes his own experiences with women, he speaks to Amory's fear: "If I start to hold somebody's hand," Kerry says, "they laugh at me, and *let* me, just as if it wasn't part of them. As soon as I get hold of a hand they sort of disconnect it from the rest of them" (TSOP, 52). Though Amory acts as if he were in a position to give advice to Kerry, he is not, as we see in a very brief flirtation he engages in during his time as a prep school student.

He begins his flirtation with Myra by attempting to elicit her concern. When she tells him that he should not be smoking, he responds, "Nobody cares." She returns, "I care." Though he is attempting to win her sympathy so that he can kiss her, it is true that his parents' concern for him is limited. He seems to be acting upon that fear when he suddenly turns away from her with "disgust" and "loathing" after she rests her head on his shoulder. He is repulsed by the thought of "their clinging hands." Like Kerry, Amory seems to be afraid that she will "disconnect" her hand from the rest of herself, that her clinging nature will give way to a desire to shun him. Not only does this comical scene hint at serious problems in his past, but it also looks forward to pressing difficulties with intimacy that he will experience in the future, difficulties that hinder his maturational progress. He repeatedly becomes involved in relationships that recall those of his childhood, and since he rarely reflects upon the reason for his behavior—he is an heir to his parents' Victorian tendency to repress emotion—he is not able to anticipate the familiar difficulties that arise.

Amory's relationship with Isabelle, which occurs when he is an undergraduate, provides further evidence that beneath his aloofness lies a fear of object loss. When she bruises herself, Amory makes light of the situation. She responds, "You're not very sympathetic" (TSOP, 89). They then argue and become angry with each other. Amory realizes that he has no affection for her, but significantly, he is still troubled by her "coldness" toward him. She observes that he lacks the "self-confidence" he has claimed to have. Their relationship ends abruptly, and though he briefly considers whether he is "temperamentally unfitted for romance" (TSOP, 92), he feels "suddenly tired of thinking" (TSOP, 93), as if he cannot bring himself to reflect upon the past at length. Though he demonstrates little sympathy for her, there are suggestions in their relationship that he does wish to see her in need of his care. He has been disappointed to find that her letters to him are "aggravatingly unsentimental," and when they attend a play and Isabelle cries "through the second act," Amory is "filled . . . with tenderness to watch her" (TSOP, 88). Amory's attraction to her weeping hints at a part of his personality that becomes evident in his next relationship with Clara, a woman who has experienced calamity.

Clara, a third cousin of Amory's, whom he meets for the first time after he has graduated from college, is recently widowed. Before he meets her, he is under the impression that she is in financial distress, and "the idea that the girl was poverty-stricken . . . appeal[s] to Amory's sense of situation" (TSOP, 131). However, he is disappointed to find that she lives in a well-maintained house and is coping emotionally with her loss. And though her husband has died only six months before, she is not in a deep state of grief, for "sorrow [lies] lightly around her" (TSOP, 131), much as his mother's melancholia has been partially hidden from him. Though she does not lean upon him for support, he attempts to imagine himself as someone who has cared for her in the past. When she shows him a poem she once wrote about a girl sitting atop a wall and thinking about the "many-colored world," he imagines Clara atop that wall, "trying to see her tragedies come marching over the gardens outside" (TSOP, 133), and he imagines himself with her. Thus, while Amory has not attempted thus far to reflect on the cause of his mother's depression, he does attempt to appreciate the past troubles of the "immemorial" Clara.

In his visits with her, he is disturbed by the fact that other men occupy her attention, and even more disturbed that she spends a great deal of time with her two children. Indeed, though she is learned and likes to socialize, her ultimate interest is in being a mother. As she admits, she is "one of those people who have no interest in anything but their children" (TSOP, 132). When others are around, he fears that she is "not anxious to see him alone" (TSOP, 131), and he finds himself "frightfully jealous of everything about Clara: of her past, of her babies, of the men and women who flocked to drink deep of her cool kindness and rest their tired minds as at an absorbing play" (TSOP, 131). In short, he fears that she is a preoccupied mother who provides nourishment and entertainment for others instead of him. When he first met her, he was surprised that she was not a "wild-haired woman with a hungry baby at her breast" (TSOP, 131). It turns out that he is the one left hungry. He agrees with Clara when she tells him, "You sink to the third hell of depression when you think you've been slighted. In fact, you haven't much self-respect" (TSOP, 134). As if to stave off anger, he idealizes her, much as "Joseph" looked upon "Mary's eternal significance" (TSOP, 137). Amory impulsively proposes marriage, and she turns him down, for she does not love him. Though he drops his characteristic aloofness in his relationship with Clara, his possessive and impulsive behavior suggests that he has not progressed significantly since his relationship with Isabelle.

In his relationship with Rosalind, Amory does allow time for mutual feelings of love to develop, but true to his old form, he initially approaches her with caution. He tells her, "I don't want to fall in love with you" (TSOP, 176). But then, "continuing coldly," he admits that he "probably will." Within days he does, and she falls in love with him as well. However, Rosalind is consciously "selfish" and ultimately lets him down when she breaks off their relationship. When the relationship ends, he is crushed and begins acting like a "baby." We cannot say, then, that Amory has matured in this relationship either.

His relationship with Eleanor, however, does demonstrate emotional progress on his part. He meets her after "losing himself entirely" while walking through the countryside, a metaphor for his loss of a narcissism, since in contrast to his behavior with Rosalind, he approaches Eleanor without caution and does not prevent himself from falling "half in love." And in contrast to his relationship with Clara, he does not idealize her. His relationship with her is the only one that is consummated, as if he no longer fears intimacy. And when their affair ends, he does not act obsessively and childishly, as he did after Rosalind broke up with him. Perhaps he is able to act this way because he feels that he will never "care as he had once cared before" he broke up with Rosalind (TSOP, 214), but there may be another reason why he achieves progress here.

In order to understand his progress, we might first reflect upon his creator. Given the fact that two of Fitzgerald's sisters died before his birth and one shortly after, it is interesting that there are references in this chapter to famous sisters in literature. Amory calls her Madeleine, a reference to the character

of the same name in Poe's "The Fall of the House of Usher,"
who haunts her brother after he "mistakenly" buries her alive.
Furthermore, when Eleanor first approaches him, she asks him
if he is Manfred, and we are reminded that Byron wrote "Manfred" in response to feelings of loss resulting after his affair
with his stepsister ended. Like these women, Eleanor maintains a haunting presence. She is "shadowy and unreal,"
"wraith-like," and "dim as a dream." A haunted atmosphere
attends Amory and Eleanor's relationship, for they spend most
of their time together outside in the nighttime darkness.

  For Fitzgerald, depicting Eleanor as an uncanny sister arising from the dead would help him to identify with the object of
his parents' grief. Now he could be closer to his parents, and
they to him. Analogously, we may view Amory's relationship
with Eleanor as Amory's identification with his mother's grief.
Accordingly, Eleanor has a sense of loss that stems from her
separation from the aristocratic, European background in
which she was raised—a feeling that has plagued Beatrice.
Though Darcy has encouraged Amory to distance himself from
others, to feel that his home is where he is not, Amory ignores
this "advice" now, for he welcomes the fact that Eleanor's
presence instills in him "a sense of coming home" (TSOP, 211).
Whereas Amory's relationship with Beatrice forced him to perform for her, with Eleanor he no longer feels "like a character
in a play" (TSOP, 211), as if empathizing with another person's
distress comes naturally to him at this point in his life. While
he seems to have maintained an air of aloof cynicism and run
off to boarding school as a way of avoiding feelings of ambivalence toward his parents, he is able to feel degrees of both love
and hate for Eleanor. Not surprisingly, it is in this chapter that
he directly looks back upon the course of his life, recognizing
its lack of progress. Importantly, his thoughts during his time
with Eleanor are unsettling. Even when he thinks of his relationship with her afterward, he can still "hear the wind sobbing around him and sending little chills into the places beside
his heart" (TSOP, 206). But if Amory is unconsciously confronting his parents' depressive, preoccupied nature in his relationship with Eleanor, then it makes sense that he would
encounter feelings of helplessness and coldness.

In truth, Amory has felt haunted before meeting Eleanor. She is not the first ghostly presence he has encountered, for there is also the revenant of Dick Humbird, who plagues Amory's conscience. Given the fact that his parents are mysteriously preoccupied with something or someone, it is not surprising that he has come to believe in the supernatural. He tells his college classmate Burne Holiday that he was not afraid of the dark as a child, but now he is, as if his unresolved attitude toward his parents' hidden life bears a more malign influence on his emotions over time. After spending many summer nights with Eleanor however, he conquers his fear of his parents' dark night of the soul. Why does his relationship with her end? He realizes that she is his "mirror," and his love diminishes. In identifying with the sisterly Eleanor, he has been seeking maternal mirroring, but now he must develop a unique sense of self to complement his filial self.

PARENTAL DEPRESSION AND GENDER IDENTITY

While his mother's depression has encouraged Amory toward a narcissistic defense, it has also invested him with an unusual sense of gender. Beatrice strives to prove she has a "masculine" constitution, boasting of the fact that any man would have been "shattered" if he had consumed as much alcohol as she has over the course of her life. In hiding her depression, she hides her "feminine" weakness. When she does admit to her "feminine" constitution, she projects the same quality onto her son. Declaring to a group of woman that her son is "delicate" she adds, "we're all delicate; *here*, you know" (TSOP, 5). He has assimilated her image of him, for he fears for his physical well-being when he first participates in sports as a child.

Beatrice's comments notwithstanding, masculinity is constructed in this novel as more delicate than femininity. Rosalind states, "Men don't know how to be really angry or really happy—and the ones that do, go to pieces" (TSOP, 162). In other words, their repressiveness ultimately hinders their ability to cope. Beatrice, who avoids expressing her feelings and medicates them through alcohol, is thus reacting against "fem-

inine" emotional sensitivity, in spite of her occasional sentimental outbursts. Accordingly, when she tells Bishop Wiston
that she does not wish to enlist his sympathy for her, she contrasts herself with the "hysterical women" who visit him. She
is more comfortable with things than with emotions, since she
has a "passion" not for socializing, but for money. She notes
that she would like to work in the world of finance if she were
a man. Her breakdowns are in keeping with the tendency of
men who feel strong emotions to "go to pieces."

Amory's desire for self-reliance, his wish to overcome all
emotional difficulties on his own, thus demonstrates "masculinity." The withdrawn Mr. Blaine and the determinedly impassive Darcy have provided Amory with examples of
"masculine" self-reliance. However, though he often succeeds
in hiding behind a shell of emotional coldness, he is also "tem-
peramental," as Rosalind's brother Alec tells her. Fittingly,
Amory "goes to pieces" after she breaks up with him. His particular difficulty in dealing with object loss at other times in
his life further accords with his "masculine" nature. Given his
underlying "feminine" nature, it is interesting that he is attracted to the Triangle (theatrical) Club at Princeton, where
the productions include "boys [acting] as girls." We are reminded of the famous publicity photograph for the Triangle
Club in which Amory's creator delightedly dressed in drag.

While Amory mirrors his mother's conflicting "masculine"
and "feminine" qualities, his girlfriends in turn mirror him.
Though he is attracted to emotionality in women, he also repeatedly involves himself with women who display an outer
facade of impassivity. Perhaps there is a hint of his preferences
when he refers to Myra as "sympatico," choosing a masculine
form of the adjective. Isabelle, for her part, apparently acts too
femininely when she complains about her bruised neck and his
insensitivity, for he tells her, "Oh don't be so darned feminine"
(TSOP, 90). Amory's next love interest, Clara, demonstrates a
feminine sensitivity in her care for her children, but she also
has a "calm virility" in overcoming her grief, a calmness Beatrice fails to achieve. Appropriately, Clara smokes cigarettes.
Amory envisions himself at one point as playing the role of Eve
to Clara's Adam, as if admitting to a role reversal. Rosalind
continues the trend, for not only does she demonstrate cool-

ness, but she is also athletic. Amory anticipates Rosalind's nature, since he says upon seeing her for the first time, "I thought you'd be sort of—sort of—sexless, you know, swim and play golf" (TSOP, 163). She does not disappoint him, for he becomes "interested" when she says, "I'm not really feminine, you know—in my mind" (TSOP, 163). Amory "delightedly" listens to an anecdote about a swimming party Rosalind once attended, in which she displayed both her impassivity and athleticism. She jumped from a very high spot into the water and then taunted a man who evinced fear in diving from the same spot. Amory's final love interest, Eleanor, resembles the previous women in his life. She has a mustache-like white line above of her lips. She resents the fact that she is supposed to find a man to support her, and she envies Amory's opportunity, as a male, to travel around the world with no emotional ties to others.

AMORY'S "SUPERCILIOUS SACRIFICE"

If Amory's relationship with Eleanor represents his first experience in confronting his parents' haunted past, then it seems appropriate that, in the next and penultimate chapter of the novel, he is able to demonstrate an outward-directed "feminine" sensitivity, to accept his caregiving role. Here Amory has traveled to the Atlantic City boardwalk, and in the wake of his failed relationships, he feels that "life ha[s] rejected him" (TSOP, 227). Both his father and mother have died at this point. Amory's visit to the ocean suggests an attempt to return to a state of natal equilibrium, to overcome his sense of rejection. He feels "lulled" by the sight of the waves. He associates the ocean with his mother, since in a previous visit there, he recalled a childhood experience of visiting the eastern coast with her.

By chance, he does find an opportunity to counter his sense of rejection. He runs into Alex, who is with a single woman. When the police seek to arrest Alex for transporting the woman across state lines "f'r immoral purp'ses," Amory voluntarily takes the blame. The police let Amory go without pressing charges, though they report the incident to the newspapers,

and Amory's name is publicly soiled. In assisting Alex, Amory
becomes a parent to him, as if accepting the caretaking role his
mother had encouraged in him. Amory "takes care" of Alex because he considers that Alex has a family—in other words, that
Alex must be rescued and permitted to become a parent again.
Amory imagines God to be speaking to him, telling him to be a
parent to Alex: "Weep not for me but for thy children" (TSOP,
229). Since we find Amory declaring "all God's dead" in the
next chapter, his perception of divine inspiration strikes us as
remarkably self-serving. Accordingly, he shows little actual
regard for Alex as a person. Amory sees his sacrifice as "super-
cilious," an "essential luxury," as if it stems from a more pressing need unrelated to the immediate circumstances. In helping
Alex, he is accepting his lifelong calling as a caretaker to Beatrice, beginning to mend his sense of maternal loss.

In the final chapter, his past continues to influence him, for
he feels a need to "escape from [his] consuming introspection
by thinking of children and the infinite possibilities of children" (TSOP, 241). Thus, he envisions offspring much as his
mother envisioned him—as someone who could rescue her
from the burden of her depression. Moreover, when he comes
to the conclusion that he represents "Beatrice's immortality,"
he conceives of himself as an Orpheus-like rescuer from the
underworld. However, later in the final chapter, his philosophical disquisition suggests his desire not to repeat the past. After
a stranger in an automobile gives Amory a lift, the latter becomes engaged in a long conversation. Amory advocates a social system encouraging parents not to spoil their children in
order to cover up past neglect:

> if the mother has spent in chasing men the years in which she
> should have been preparing herself to educate her children—so
> much the worse for the child. He shouldn't be artificially bolstered
> up with money, sent to these horrible tutoring schools, dragged
> through college. . . . Every boy ought to have an equal start. (TSOP,
> 252)

Amory's espousal of a system in which the neglected child
should remain neglected is harsh, apparently a knee-jerk reaction against the way Beatrice's pampering of him concealed

her underempathy. Amory again demonstrates his conflicted attitude toward the past when he resolves to become more charitable in the future, even though he feels that he lacks a maternal sensitivity to others, that he does not have "one drop of the milk of human kindness" (TSOP, 258). Thus, his desire to take care of others remains only a compulsion.

ROMANTICISM AND SENTIMENTALISM

Amory's grudging acceptance of a caregiving role parallels his ambivalent attitude toward sentimentalism and romanticism, two philosophies that militated against the ethos of industrialization and progress in the nineteenth century. To understand Amory's view on these philosophies, it is helpful for us to consider an epigram he is fond of repeating: "the sentimental person thinks things will last—the romantic person has a desperate confidence that they won't" (TSOP, 212). In other words, the sentimentalist denies loss, while the romanticist delights in it. In comparing the two perspectives, he also notes, "Sentiment is emotion." Though he does not elaborate on this comment, he is probably suggesting that the sentimentalist exaggerates feelings toward the past in order to keep the past alive. Although the sentimental and romantic traditions are not so clearly distinct from each other, what is important here is that Amory is struggling to preserve a dichotomy between the two in repeating the epigram. Consequently, his definition illuminates his feelings toward the two traditions throughout the novel.

As a child of the twentieth century, Amory does not fully accept either tradition. In the modernist era, intellectuals felt that both modes of thought had shielded people from the harsh reality finally made manifest by the Great War. At the end of the novel, Amory expresses disillusionment in the face of the "Victorian war," as he refers to it, and he ridicules romanticism and sentimentalism. He attacks the "mediocre intellects" who "use the remnants of romantic chivalry, diluted with Victorian sentiment" (TSOP, 220). Moreover, he derides Rupert Brooke and Byron as "flaneurs" and "poseurs." However, Amory is not completely critical of these past modes of perception. As if identifying with his mother's sentimentalism and his father's Byronic romanticism, he wavers between the two traditions.

At first he tilts toward a romantic view of loss, for he embraces thoughts of death. After arriving late for Myra's party, he "romance[s]," claiming falsely that he got into an auto accident when riding with his uncle and aunt. When she asks if anyone was killed, he leads her to believe at first that one of his relatives died in the crash. Later, he considers attending Andover or Exeter, "with their memories of New England dead" (TSOP, 29). His fascination with death occurs when the world war commences, and he "hope[s] that it [will] be long and bloody" (TSOP, 58). He delights in loss, thus allowing himself to become numbed to reality, much as he displays a "masculine" desire to overcome all obstacles, to remain self-reliant.

Early on in his life, he tends not to demonstrate sentimentality, since he resists "feminine" sensitivity. He appears to be aware of the traditional link between sentimentality and femininity, for when Rosalind demonstrates the sentimentalist tendency to focus on the bright aspects of her past as a denial of loss, Amory suggests that men cannot do the same. In breaking up with him, she states that she will preserve their experiences "as a beautiful memory—tucked away in [her] heart," and he responds, "Yes, women can do that—but not men" (TSOP, 181). Eventually, however, his attitude toward loss changes, for he begins to experience feelings of grief that often resemble the intense emotion of sentimentalism.

He experiences several losses in his life during his adolescence—the deaths of Darcy, Humbird, and two other college classmates in the war, his break-up with Rosalind, and financial loss—that would foster his identification with his mother's sentimentalism.[5] Though he does not outwardly demonstrate a profound sense of loss over his mother's death, perhaps he does mourn for her, a process that would further encourage his identification with her. For Freud, mourning involves the introjection of the lost love object into the ego.[6] After his breakup with Rosalind, he gets caught up in an "ecstasy of sentiment." He becomes preoccupied with past happiness and oblivious to present reality, as demonstrated by his determination to "celebrate" by drinking, and his use of the present perfect tense to describe his relationship with her: "We've been so happy, so very happy . . ." (TSOP, 188). He lives in the past, denying the reality of loss. Darcy suspects that the war and the relationship with Rosalind have led Amory to become sentimental, for after referring in a letter to the break-up, Darcy laments, "you have lost all the feeling of romance that you had before the war" (TSOP, 220).

At the beginning of the Eleanor episode, she suspects that he is a romantic, for she has overheard him reciting Poe, and when she asks him if he is Manfred, she appears to be wondering if he shares Manfred's romantic belief in his soul's transcendence of death anxiety. However, she later suspects that he may instead be a sentimentalist, for she asks him if he is Queen Victoria, a woman who served as a prominent beacon of sentimental grief. Victoria embodied the "sentimental" desire to preserve the past, for she retained the possessions of her late husband throughout her entire life. In response to Eleanor's intimations—she later accuses him outright of being a sentimentalist—Amory tells her that he is in fact Don Juan, as if eager at this point to share Don Juan's numbness to object loss.

However, since his relationship with Eleanor leads him toward emotional growth, it is fitting that after their relationships ends, four particular incidents in his life demonstrate that he is learning to confront his sense of loss. First, he recalls a time in New York City when he witnessed a delivery boy carrying a funeral wreath into the subway, an act that "had suddenly cleared the air and given every one in the car a momentary glow" (TSOP, 237). Later, his feeling of "haunting grief" at Darcy's funeral serves as another step in his progression. Still later, at the end of the scene in which he has his conversation with the stranger in the automobile, Amory realizes that the stranger is the father of Jesse Ferrenby, one of Amory's classmates who was killed in the war. Amory suddenly feels a strong bond with Mr. Ferrenby, whom we can see as a surrogate for his grieving parents.

Amory attains his greatest sense of the importance of loss when he visits a cemetery in the penultimate passage of the novel. In order to capture the spirit of this scene, it will be necessary for me to quote the scene in full:

The afternoon waned from the purging good of three o'clock to the golden beauty of four. Afterwards he walked through the dull ache of a setting sun when even the clouds seemed bleeding and at twilight he came to a graveyard. There was a dusky, dreamy smell of flowers and the ghost of a new moon in the sky and shadows everywhere. On an impulse he considered trying to open the door of a rusty iron vault built into the side of a hill; a vault washed clean and covered with late-blooming, weepy watery-blue flowers that might have grown from dead eyes, sticky to the touch with a sickening odor.

Amory wanted to *feel* "William Dayfield, 1864."

He wondered that graves ever made people consider life in vain; somehow he could find nothing hopeless in having lived. All the broken columns and clasped hands and doves and angels meant romances. He fancied that in a hundred years he would like having young people speculate as to whether his eyes were brown or blue, and he hoped quite passionately that his grave would have about it an air of many, many years ago. It seemed strange that out of a row of Union soldiers two or three made him think of dead loves and dead lovers, when they were exactly like the rest, even to the yellowish moss. (TSOP, 259–60)

In this passage, as well as in his recollection of the funeral wreath on the subway, in his attendance of Darcy's funeral, and in his encounter with Jesse Ferrenby's father, Amory does not feel the modernist sense of emptiness in the face of death. Rather, there is a touch of romanticism in his thoughts, for death provides him with a sense of excitement, as in romantic literature. His thoughts also bear a resemblance to sentimentalism. In sentimental literature, death provides people with a sense of connectedness to others, as it does for Amory, who feels closer to Jesse Ferrenby, Mr. Ferrenby, and William Dayfield. If the sentimentalist focuses on the bright side of life, then Amory does so when he concludes that he can "find nothing hopeless in having lived." And if "sentiment is emotion," then we can see that Amory's desire to "*feel* William Dayfield," as if he were still alive, is in keeping with that tradition.

A letter Fitzgerald wrote in 1940 to the movie producer Lester Cowan helps us to understand the sentimental strain in this passage. In discussing the movie treatment for his short story "Babylon Revisited," Fitzgerald writes that "though no one is more responsive than I am to true sentiment and emotion, I still hold out against any sentimentality."[7] Fitzgerald's statement suggests his agreement with one made by Rosalind: "I want sentiment—real sentiment." We can infer that Rosalind would consider Amory's thoughts in the graveyard to be an example of "real sentiment," for her character is based on Zelda, and Zelda deserves credit for writing this passage of the novel. Fitzgerald culled the passage nearly verbatim from a letter she had written describing her own experiences. Thus, in expressing "true" or "real" sentiment, Amory has accepted a form of "unmanly" sensitivity. He is thus no longer neglecting his heart, as his mother would say. Though he has shown insensitivity to the grief of his parents and of Victorians in general, and has resisted grief and thoughts of the past himself, he now embraces his parents' romanticism and sentimentalism. In the final passage of the novel, he does demonstrate a marked sense of disillusion when he criticizes the "old creeds," but ultimately he decides not to turn his back on the past.

Note that we see no sign that Amory is consciously thinking of his capacity for "feminine" sensitivity at the end of the novel. Moreover, there is no evidence that he recognizes the grieving Mr. Ferrenby as a stand-in for his parents, or that he is aware of the link between his romanticism and sentimentalism and the perspectives of his parents. The closest he comes to thinking consciously of Beatrice and Stephen is when he resolves "to use to the utmost himself and his *heritage*" (TSOP, 282; emphasis mine) in order to succeed in life. We cannot agree with him, then, when he declares "I know myself" in the last sentence of the novel. He has achieved progress, but without a conscious understanding of the relationship between his childhood and his present life, he may well continue to struggle with self-love and love for others.

4

The Beautiful and Damned and Feminine Occultism: Fitzgerald's Attraction-Repulsion to Mourning

What is he, whose grief
Bears such an emphasis? whose phrase of sorrow
Conjures the wand'ring stars, and makes them stand
Like wonder-wounded hearers?

—Hamlet

Shakespeare was a Bilphist [*sic*]. . . .
If you've read *Hamlet* you can't help but see.
—Mrs. Gilbert, *The Beautiful and Damned*

The beautiful and damned, fitzgerald's second and least-known novel, burlesques the decline of Anthony Patch. Fraught with a sense of the meaninglessness of life, Anthony lacks the motivation to devote himself to a profession. As if un-manned, he lives off his mother's modest inheritance. He antic-ipates that he will soon come into the much larger inheritance of his grandfather, the Wall Street tycoon and zealously puri-tanical reformist Adam Patch. Anthony marries Gloria Gil-bert, and the two spend much time in drunken revels with Maury Noble and Richard Caramel, the former a devout cynic, the latter a writer who becomes increasingly middlebrow with each new work. After Anthony's ascetic grandfather stumbles upon one of Anthony's parties, he writes Anthony out of his will. Anthony and Gloria then contest it. Meanwhile, Anthony drinks more and more and becomes increasingly distanced from and bitter toward his wife. When the two finally win their lawsuit, Anthony has become physically feeble and a border-line psychotic. He remains unrepentant, while Gloria apparently stays with him only for his money. Evidently, the two are damned.

Readers of the novel will readily see its autobiographical roots, its transplantation of Fitzgerald and Zelda's reckless behavior. Yet one particular aspect of the novel is less clearly an offshoot of Fitzgerald's life: his parents' half-buried grief and his resultant experience with parental deprivation as an infant. These themes, previously found in Amory's childhood in *This Side of Paradise*, also parallel events in Anthony's childhood, for he is an orphan raised by his grieving grandfather. Though at least before his "crack-up," Fitzgerald did not outwardly demonstrate a sense of anomie similar to his fictional protagonist's, the novelist's related childhood experiences would have fostered the insight provided into the etiology of Anthony's anomie, for Anthony's upbringing underlies his emotional troubles. Moreover, Fitzgerald's relationship with Zelda's family informs his portrayal of Gloria and her familial background. While Zelda and her mother were interested in theosophy and spiritualism, Mrs. Gilbert visits a palmist and believes in "Bilphism" (Fitzgerald's coinage), a religion Gloria feels strongly drawn to as well. Mrs. Gilbert describes Bilphism as the "science of all religions," a claim believers made of theosophy.[1] Bilphism, like spiritualism and theosophy, is a female-dominated religion.

We recall that Mrs. Sayre's unresolved grief very likely contributed to her occult leanings, since spiritualistic seances of course appeal particularly to those in bereavement, while theosophy, influenced by astrology, Hinduism, and other beliefs, provides a map of the afterworld sought by participants in seances. Interestingly, Maury observes at one point that Mrs. Gilbert and her husband are "as sad as professional mourners" (BD, 49). For an unsympathetic observer such as Maury, others' underlying grief might well appear theatrical. Whatever has prompted Mrs. Gilbert to turn to Bilphism, we can see a parallel between the religion's appeal to those in bereavement and Anthony's experience of parental loss, a parallel that Fitzgerald develops in the novel.

Anthony harbors conflicting feelings toward his wife's religious upbringing. Bilphism places in full view the anxiety-provoking issues of death, mourning, and the afterworld—issues that he attempts to avoid by clinging to his nihilism. Accordingly, he adheres to the norm of impassivity among the male characters in the novel by mocking Bilphism, including its appeal to distraught women. At the same time, however, Gloria's Bilphistic nature also underlies much of his attraction to her. And often his perspective upon life mirrors the religion's philosophy. An analysis of his affinity for Bilphism provides us with an altered perspective on the overall meaning of the novel. James E. Miller notes that *The Beautiful and Damned* "is concerned with Anthony and Gloria's rejection of the kind of [ascetic] life Grandfather Patch symbolizes," but he also observes that their rebelliousness is negated: the "theme of the meaninglessness of life tends to neutralize the theme of revolt."[2] While Miller insightfully points out a thematic contradiction, one important motif of revolt does alter the fundamental meaning of the novel. Anthony's attraction to the "unmanly" grief Gloria embodies serves implicitly as a resistance to his grandfather's "masculine" rigidity, a subversion of the normative gender roles of society as a whole. To be sure, however, eventually this motif of revolt is also weakened. The ending of the novel militates against the preceding parts, for Fitzgerald's suggestion of Gloria's unfortunate fate does not accord with his previous depiction of her gradual but noteworthy development of the ability to mourn.

THE HOUSE OF MOURNING

The conflict between normative gender roles and the need to mourn emerges in the first chapter of the novel. In sketching out this conflict, Fitzgerald shows one area of his development as a writer, for he provides a more convincing portrait of his protagonist's difficult childhood than he had provided of Amory Blaine's. He does so even though the burlesque aspect of *The Beautiful and Damned* allows for a less sympathetic depiction of the protagonist than is called for in the bildungsroman form of *This Side of Paradise*. The nature of the parent-child disharmony is clouded over in Fitzgerald's first novel, since we do not know why his mother is depressed and his father remote. Consequently, Amory's later teenage angst, seen only in a societal light, might not appear thoroughly convincing. In contrast, we can more easily gain a sense of how Anthony's angst develops. The account of his familial history begins with his grandfather. After returning from the Civil War, Grandfather Patch "charged into Wall Street" (BD, 4), married, and had a son named Ulysses. The narrative then skips to Ulysses's marriage, the birth of Anthony, and the death of Anthony's mother five years later. Likely numbed by grief, Ulysses would visit Anthony's nursery daily for "as much as an hour" (BD, 6)—the narrator's sarcastic suggestion that Anthony's father would spend little time with his son at all. Ulysses "was continually promising Anthony hunting trips and fishing trips and excursions to Atlantic City, 'oh, some time soon now'; but none of them ever materialized" (BD, 6). Like his ancient Greek namesake, Ulysses appears to have been torn between the desire to remain apart from his wife and son or to redirect his thoughts toward them. Eventually, Anthony's father did attempt a return home, for he finally took his son on a trip to Europe, a place emblematic of the Patchs' old world, their familial past. However, to Anthony's "despair," his father suddenly took sick and died there. Not long after, his grandmother died, though she was never a significant presence in his life, leaving him to be raised by Grandfather Patch only, whose "thoughts ran a great deal on the Civil War, somewhat on his dead wife and son, almost infinitesimally on his grandson Anthony" (BD, 4–5).

Thus, from the age of five, Anthony was raised by adults preoccupied with grief—first his father, then his grandfather. Or rather, in "charging into" his business career after the war, Grandfather Patch appears to have been preoccupied with avoiding his grief, with blindly pursuing Victorian progress instead of taking time to reflect upon the casualties of war. Moreover, though he wishes to oversee the "moral regeneration of the world" (BD, 4), as if to ensure his own regeneration in the next world, we do not gain the sense that he focuses upon his own morality. We gain a glimpse into his avoidance of the personal after he tells Anthony at one point, "I think a great deal about the after-life" (BD, 140). He then reminisces momentarily about his sister, who is evidently dead now, and then breaks off that topic by returning to the subject of the afterlife, as if to avoid facing his ambivalence toward her, confronting his grief. Of course eschatological consideration can also cause anxiety, and it is most likely for this reason that he then interrupts himself again and alters the expression on his face, "his entire personality seem[ing] to snap together like a trap" (BD, 140). Previously in this scene, he has shown similarly repressed feelings for his deceased son. In offering his home as a site for Anthony's wedding to Gloria, he mistakenly recalls that his son had been married there too. Anthony finds himself feeling "strangely sorry" for Grandfather Patch, since the man "had forgotten something about his son's wedding that he should have remembered" (BD, 141). Apparently, Grandfather Patch has spent little time sorting through his memories of his lost son.

Anthony's few recollections of his childhood do not immediately indicate he has strong feelings about the way he was raised. He remembers his father's manners—Ulysses's "gallant" behavior—and he has "nebulous" memories of his mother, "the Boston Society Contralto," performing sometimes for company, sometimes for him alone. Anthony's recollection of only these details suggests that he remembers the appearance his parents put on for the outside world, the shell of their personality. As if attempting during his childhood to see beneath the surface, Anthony repeatedly gazed upon a photograph in his bedroom of his parents and himself, in which the three of them stand in a traditional pose, dressed in their best clothes. Anthony has apparently been unable to see in the formal photograph what he is looking for, since it has "acquired the impersonality of furniture" in his adulthood. Or more literally, in the face of his frustrated attempts to remember them, he instead assumes an air of "impersonality," indifference, toward them. His attempted indifference thus resembles his grandfather's avoidance of grief.

Anthony's attitude carries over into the rest of his life, for he distances himself from others, finding solace during his childhood in reading and stamp collecting. When he grows up and enters Harvard, "he had lived almost entirely within himself" (BD, 7). Though he takes up a more active social life in his senior year in college, "that long adolescent aloofness and consequent shyness still dictate[s] to his conduct" (BD, 9). As we would expect, separating himself from others has not curtailed the pain of parental loss, for he becomes "wedded to a vague melancholy that was to stay beside him through the rest of his life" (BD, 6). He has felt haunted since his youth: "At eleven he had a horror of death. Within six impressionable years his parents had died and his grandmother had faded off almost imperceptibly. . . . So to Anthony life was a struggle against death, that waited at every corner" (BD, 6–7). Unlike a tragic character for whom the presence of death ultimately increases his or her sense of responsibility, Anthony's attempt to remain aloof and indifferent to the presence of death and loss leads to his ironic sense of absurdity, a flimsy defense against grief. He feels he has "inherited only the vast tradition of human failure—that, and the sense of death" (BD, 218). His belief in life's absurdity yields a self-destructive impulse, as we see most clearly when he tells Gloria that he wants to get killed in the Great War after learning he has been drafted. Though the fighting ends before he goes overseas, his self-destructiveness manifests itself in his financial recklessness and careless behavior throughout his life.

Anthony and Grandfather Patch's unwillingness to confront their grief is characteristic in the novel of men in general. Mr. Gilbert, Gloria's father, displays "masculine impassivity," responding without emotion to everything his wife says, periodically uttering "yes—yes—yes—yes," as if attempting to shush her. Anthony fears the possibility that his own "feminine" emotion cannot be repressed, for he feels frightened one night upon hearing the sound coming from outside his apartment of an "hysterical" female crying, her voice only briefly interrupted by the "low rumble of a man's voice" (BD, 149). For Anthony, the woman's persistent crying represents his own persistent "feminine" need to grieve, since we see through interior monologue that he associates her voice with life as a whole, including apparently his own: "Life was that sound out there, that ghastly reiterated female sound" (BD, 150). Anthony wishes that he could be "miles above," that he could avoid the unmanning pain of life.

Even though he assumes an air of masculine impassivity, he would likely wish at the same time to avoid such a pose, since it underlies his melancholic nature. Accordingly, his interest in

becoming an historian implicitly represents a desire to resist
the normative gender roles in his family and society. He tells
his grandfather that he aspires to write a history of the Middle
Ages, and though he says so in the hope that his grandfather
will envision him as an upright young man deserving of the
Patch inheritance, his statement speaks on a symbolic level to
his inner need to confront the middle years of his childhood,
the time when he lost his mother and father. He too has a dual,
Ulysses-like attitude toward his past.

Indeed, sincerity underlies his statement, for we are later
told that "some unwelcome survival of a fetish had drawn him
three weeks before down to the public library, where . . . he had
drawn out half a dozen books on the Italian Renaissance" (BD,
54). In referring to the fetishistic nature of the books, Fitzgerald is alluding not to the Freudian fetish, but rather to the supernatural belief that certain objects, "fetishes," are inhabited
by spirits. Because they promise the proximity of the spiritual
world, they contain a magical allure. Fitzgerald may have had
in mind here the practice of "spirit writing," or "automatic
writing," a fundamental aspect of the seance in which the medium transcribes words purportedly dictated by a deceased
person. Much as Anthony's avid reading habits served him as a
child, his "fetish" for writing history serves a therapeutic role,
providing him with an opportunity to reconstruct his understanding of the world.

Eventually he publishes an essay on Florentine history.
However, he never publishes any other historical works, and
he ceases his avid reading habits, symptoms of his opposing desire to avoid confronting his past, to withdraw from life in general. A similar abandonment of the creative impulse occurs
several years into his marriage, when he tries his hand at fiction writing. Though he does so only in a desperate and rare
attempt to make money, the plot of one of his stories, like the
library books on European history, relates to his personal life.
Richard's best selling fiction is read by teary-eyed women, and
Anthony's story, "The Little Open Doors," also seems designed
to speak to female readers' grief. It involves the "occult: an estranged couple were brought together by a medium in a vaude-
ville show" (BD, 302). Thus, the feminine world of the occult
serves to repair the couple's sense of loss, much as the medium

contacts sitters' deceased loved ones in seances. Anthony's lack of enthusiasm in writing the story demonstrates his lack of awareness, or "masculine" disavowal, of its autobiographical nature, for his experiences with loss likely influence his writing of the story. As we shall see, Gloria has displayed a medium-like ability to alleviate his feelings of grief, in spite of his ambivalence toward her.

BILPHISM: CONTACTING THE AFTERWORLD

Throughout their relationship, Gloria acts like a supernatural fetish upon him, attracting and repelling him with her seeming promise as a link to the afterworld. Fitzgerald appears to have been uncertain about what point of view to assume in depicting Gloria. He begins the novel with caricature, for Gloria is uncomplimentarily associated early on with various malign beings, including sirens, vampires, and ancient sorceresses. Given her religious background, and Fitzgerald's later depiction of Myrtle Wilson in *The Great Gatsby* as presiding over a seance, we might think of Gloria's enchanting role as that of a modern spiritualistic medium. The Keatsian title for a draft of Fitzgerald's novel—"The Beautiful Woman without Mercy"—provides an indication that he initially attached great importance to Gloria's role in demonically paralyzing Anthony, in precipitating his decline. Despite or because of the fact that her mercilessness was considered important, Fitzgerald intended to marginalize her role in the novel. Henry Dan Piper has observed that initially "Gloria was intended to take a back seat" and serve as a "more humorous character."[3] However, Piper also observes that in the final draft, she becomes "the most vital and consistently interesting person in the novel."[4] Indeed, she no longer appears as the stereotypical manipulative woman at the end, for she has little effect upon Anthony's decline. He becomes his own antagonist. In fact, the rate of his decline accelerates as he distances himself from Gloria and her increasing predilection for the occult.

When she first visits his apartment, a place "to conjure with," the "magician-like" Anthony attempts to create an aura of enchantment as he turns on a lamp casting a glow of "glory."

Soon, however, Gloria displays a power to conjure with him. The narrator links her through allusion to several enchantresses, such as "Zuleika the Conjurer." Zuleika Dobson, the eponymous character of Max Beerbohm's 1910 burlesque, performs only cheap magic tricks before audiences, yet she seems to be a great magician in another sense, for such physical allure emanates from her person that every man instantly falls in love with her at first sight, as if under a spell. Even the duke falls for her, in spite of his attempts to appear aloof. Like the duke, Anthony fails to remain emotionally detached. In successive sections of the novel entitled, fittingly, "Magic" and "Black Magic," Anthony suddenly feels as if he has fallen under her control, and he then quarrels with her about her lack of reciprocal devotion to him. He finds that a mystical force has drawn him toward her, some "emotion that was neither mental nor physical, nor merely a mixture of the two" (BD, 104). He has become "a passive thing, acted upon by an influence above and beyond Gloria" (BD, 105). As a result of her "charm," he feels "haunted." It seems to him as if "emotion rose no longer in his breast unless she saw fit to pull an omnipotent controlling thread" (BD, 112). In an apparent reaction to his loss of control, he has a sadistic need to get back at her: "his wild thoughts varied between a passionate desire for her kisses and an equally passionate craving to hurt and mar her" (BD, 116). Though the narrator goes on to suggest that Anthony's desire for control also takes a less-violent form, that Anthony craves "in finer fashion" to "possess the triumphant soul" of Gloria, he acts physically coercive and emotionally abusive in his marriage to her.

When they marry, the magical spell over their relationship continues, for the two experience an "almost uncanny pull at each other's hearts" (BD, 168), a pull that recalls the Freudian uncanny. Though Freud believed in the validity of parapsychology, his essay "The Uncanny," as we recall from chapter 1, provides a psychoanalytic explanation for why certain occurrences provoke in us a particularly strong anxiety. Freud finds that the "uncanny is in reality nothing new or foreign, but something which is familiar and old-established in the mind that has become estranged only through the process of repression."[5] Accordingly, while Anthony "estranges" himself from the world, shrinking from life and death, Gloria reawakens his emotional investment in life and hence, makes more immediate his repressed fear of death. She has a tremendous vitality and thus seems at first to transcend the problem of mortality. A teenager when Anthony first meets her, the "heavenly" Gloria strikes him as the "most living person he ha[s] ever seen" (BD, 58). As a result, she seems to straddle the ages, appearing "very young and very old" (BD, 60), a "female Methuselah" (BD, 61). Later, in her presence, he feels "young now as he would never be again, and more triumphant than death" (BD, 126), as if through her he has temporarily mastered his uncanny fear of death. However, this last thought indicates that his intimations of immortality will eventually vanish. Indeed, in a Keatsian reverie, Anthony considers some time after their marriage, "Even Gloria's beauty needed wild emotions, needed poignancy, needed death" (BD, 214). He thus recognizes that her beauty is dependent upon her mortality rather than triumphant over it. It is soon after that he is tortured by the feeling that he has "inherited" a sense of "human failure" and a "sense of death."

Gloria's beauty exposes Anthony to his repressed emotions, and her religious background draws out his inner self. Accordingly, he demonstrates an attraction-repulsion to her Bilphistic nature. He professes his repulsion to Bilphism several years into his marriage, when she discloses the fact that she has become a devotee of the religion. He registers disgust with her, alleging that Bilphism provides for a "silly rule of reincarnation." She replies that Bilphism provides her with a sense of meaning in her life, to which he responds that religion, particularly Bilphism, stems from an unmanly evasion of hard facts: "And if you must have a faith to soften things"—he says to her—"take up [a belief] that appeals to the reason of someone besides a lot of hysterical women" (BD, 303–304). His unease with the femininity of Bilphism reminds us of his grandfather's discomfort in thinking of the afterlife.

Nevertheless, Anthony seems disturbed by the fact that she has made a full conversion to the allegedly "soft" religion of "hysterical women" instead of continuing to dabble in it. He has known of her Bilphistic predilection from the beginning of their relationship and actually betrays an attraction to that quality in her. When they are engaged, she displays her interest, opining "uncertainly": "mother says that two souls are sometimes created together and—and in love before they're born" (BD, 131). Gloria's statement resembles Zelda's theosophical rationale for marrying Fitzgerald. In response to her suggestion of reincarnated love, he lifts his head toward the ceiling, laughs patronizingly, and continues the conversation joyfully, apparently finding this statement by Bilphism's "easiest convert" to be endearing.

At the early stages of her relationship with him, Gloria keeps in check her "feminine" Bilphism, for she retains her "almost masculine," "anaesthetic" nature, a complement to her "boyish" figure. She distrusts women, suspecting they are not "clean" and "slick," her way of describing people with "solidity and strength," who go through life unconcerned and untroubled by the world around them. Of her two female friends, both display a "masculine" lack of sympathy for others. The first, Muriel Kane, is a "picker up and thrower away of men" (BD, 95), while the second, Rachael Jerryl, in no way resembles her biblical namesake, for she does not mourn when she goes from one man to the next over the course of the novel. Though Gloria has an uncanny way of bringing out Anthony's inner feelings, her emotional nature is largely repressed as well. As long as she remains this way, Anthony feels more drawn toward her than repelled. "You've got a mind like mine" he says to her when she tells him of her preference for male friendship over female. "Not strongly gendered either way" (BD, 134).

Indeed, he does have a mind like hers, for his desire for impassiveness is opposed by his occasional flights of fantasy. Though he patronizes Gloria's religion of allegedly "hysterical women," he fantasizes about the possibility of reincarnated love. His Buddhist lexicon—he envisions himself as an "epicurus in Nirvana" and views the South, where he attends boot camp, as "some warm primitive Nirvana" (BD, 337)[6]—hints at his deeper interest in existential matters, which we see in a passage of interior monologue providing Anthony's thoughts while walking with Gloria in Manhattan:

> both were walking alone in a dispassionate garden with a ghost found in a dream.

> . . . Halcyon days like boats drifting along slow-moving rivers;
> spring evenings full of a plaintive melancholy that made the past
> beautiful and bitter, bidding them look back and see that the loves
> of other summers long gone were dead with the forgotten waltzes
> of their years. (BD, 137)

His interest in the spirit world was also on display in a previous passage, when he was beginning to fall in love with Gloria. There, a "gorgeous sentiment" came over him momentarily, and he thought, "Surely the freshness of her cheeks was a gossamer projection from a land of delicate and undiscovered shades" (BD, 71). In patronizing the theory that two souls can be in love before they are born, and in ridiculing Gloria's interest in Bilphism's "silly rule of reincarnation," Anthony mocks a concern very close to his own, one most likely related to the loss of love in his childhood.

When they travel outside of New York City after their marriage, Anthony continues to show an attraction to the conflicting Bilphistic and "masculine" sides of Gloria's personality. During a visit to General Lee's home at Arlington, Gloria becomes incensed upon seeing that the home has been preserved as a tourist attraction. Offsetting her concern for the past with a "masculine" desire to move onward, she states that "just as any period decays in our minds, the things of that period should decay too" (BD, 166). Extending the subject of discussion, she criticizes those who attempt to preserve the graveyard at Tarrytown. She insists, "Sleepy Hollow's gone; Washington Irving's dead" (BD, 166). Returning to her thoughts on General Lee's home, she states, "It's just because I love the past that I want . . . its stairs to creak as if to the footsteps of women with hoop skirts and men in boots and spurs. But they've made it into a blondined, rouged-up old woman of sixty" (BD, 167). As someone with a queenly personality, Gloria probably yearns for the chivalric order of the Old South, yet her pejorative vision of the old woman demonstrates her desire not to become thoroughly enmeshed in "feminine" grief. As Anthony does not respond, apparently he shares her desire. Her reference to Tarrytown would relate directly to his life, for he grew up there. Like an Irving character—Rip Van Winkle, for example—he remains trapped between the past and the present.

The house they decide to rent outside New York City after their marriage embodies their mixed attitude toward mourning, for the pre-Revolutionary structure, in spite of some renovation, has "defiantly remained" colonial. No "blondined" and "rouged-up" mourner has attempted to preserve its past. However, Gloria becomes frightened when their servant—who is, significantly, a woman—displays intense grief. After Gloria sees the woman "weeping violently" for some reason one day, Gloria experiences an "uncanny fear." Here occurs another example of the Freudian uncanny, of a return of the repressed. After witnessing the servant's "untold and esoteric grief" (BD, 186), Gloria becomes so frightened that she cannot approach her.

Gloria's response to the presence of death, like Anthony's, has been handed down through the family, as Anthony learns:

> Gloria's penchant for premonitions and her bursts of vague supernaturalism were a surprise to Anthony. Either some complex, properly and scientifically inhibited in the early years with her Bilphistic mother, or some inherited hyper-sensitiveness, made her susceptible to any suggestion of the psychic, and, far from gullible about the motives of people, she was inclined to credit any extraordinary happening attributed to the whimsical perambulations of the buried. The desperate squeakings about the old house on windy nights that to Anthony were burglars with revolvers ready in hand represented to Gloria the auras, evil and restive, of dead generations, expiating the inexpiable upon the ancient and romantic hearth. One night, because of two swift bangs downstairs, which Anthony fearfully but unavailingly investigated, they lay awake nearly until dawn asking each other examination paper-questions about the history of the world. (BD, 187)

Thus, though she may have a phobic reaction to grave middle-aged women such as her mother, Mrs. Gilbert's religiousness has previously helped Gloria deal with her fear of death; Bilphism has "properly and scientifically inhibited" (sublimated?) it. Now that she is away from her mother, her fear returns. Significantly, by staying up all night to discuss history with Gloria—another appearance of the history leitmotif—Anthony again displays his ability to identify with her superstitiousness. In fact, his fear of burglars resembles her fear of poltergeists. His fear could be seen as a displacement of his "hypochondriacal imagination," his childhood belief that death "waited at every corner." In conversing throughout the night with her, Anthony is dealing with his fears.

All of Anthony and Gloria's flirtations with a Bilphistic-like supernaturalism during the early stages of their marriage prove therapeutic for him, as we see by the title of the chapter describing this time in his life: "The Radiant Hour." Her eventual conversion to Bilphism troubles him, however. Now she has gone too far. He previously had a chance to observe that Mrs. Gilbert deployed her spirituality as a conversational weapon, gravely observing in every conversation whether some person had a "young soul" or an old one, thus foisting her emotions upon whomever was present. Visitors were caught in the crossfire of the mutual "guerrilla warfare" waged between Mr. and Mrs. Gilbert, for her comments countered the impassive Mr. Gilbert's yesses, responses that made him a "bore and bully [of his wife's] human soul" (BD, 190). Her combativeness made her "masculine"—the "faintest white mustache" could be seen on her face.

Anthony likely fears such an advanced power struggle in his marriage. Moreover, his difficulty in accepting Gloria's Bilphism may be intensified by the fact that it occurs in the immediate aftermath of her parents' deaths. She has just attended her father's funeral, and her mother died the previous month. For Anthony, her experiences with parental loss may evoke his childhood experiences too vividly, ones from which he has attempted to distance himself.

LOSS AND BIGOTRY

In addition to his crumbling marriage, Anthony's increasingly bigoted nature marks his decline and damnation. His upbringing subtends this problem as well, for as a result of his father and grandfather's preoccupation with avoiding grief, Anthony has grown up "entirely within himself, an inarticulate boy, *thoroughly un-American*, and politely bewildered by his contemporaries" (BD, 7; emphasis mine). Thus, from his experience of familial otherness, his upbringing among adults preoccupied with grief, he clings to a sense of his superiority, holds an unegalitarian view of humanity. In *The Great Gatsby*, Fitzgerald will depict a similar psychosocial pattern, for Gatsby will struggle to maintain his belief in his godliness, in his "Platonic conception of himself," instead of accepting rejection by bluebloods grieving for the past.

However, while we admire Gatsby in his struggle for superiority over the brutish Tom Buchanan, Anthony vies with Joseph Bloeckman, who is clearly depicted as a likable character. In fact, Bloeckman, unlike Anthony, is the truly admirable outsider, for his ability to rise up in society anticipates Monroe Stahr's heroic success as a parvenu in *The Last Tycoon*. Fitzgerald takes pains to portray Bloeckman in a positive light. A New York Jew, Bloeckman resembles the "Middle Western farmer," has the self-conscious courteousness "of all good Americans" (BD, 94), and is repeatedly referred to as "dignified." Anthony, though, treats him with animus from the beginning of their acquaintanceship.[7]

Since Anthony's bigotry is linked with his sense of familial otherness, it is appropriate that Bloeckman serves as a parental figure in the novel. Bloeckman is an older man than Anthony and is closely associated with both grandfather Patch and Mr. Gilbert. As an ambitious businessman, Bloeckman repeatedly expresses his respect for Anthony's Grandfather. Moreover, in his work for a movie studio, he does business with Mr. Gilbert, an employee of a celluloid company. And while Grandfather Patch succeeded in life despite experiencing losses, Joseph Bloeckman, like his biblical namesake, has succeeded after encountering hardships in life—he worked as a peanut vendor after immigrating to America. In fact, Anthony might see Bloeckman as a more enviable version of Grandfather Patch, for while the latter represses his emotions and thus seems perpetually unhappy, the former seems to bury his past only in a public sense, for he assimilates, acquiring greater social sophistication and eventually changing his name to Black.

When both Anthony and Bloeckman court Gloria in the first book of the novel, Anthony displays a primal rage, becoming "childishly frantic" and feeling a desire to "kill" him. If Anthony's frequent thoughts of receiving Adam Patch's inheritance indicate in part a murderous wish against his unempathic grandfather, then his homicidal feelings toward the paternal Bloeckman, which are referred to as "childish," suggest a transference of aggression. His murderous wish foreshadows events at the end of the novel.

ANTHONY'S REGRESSION

By the end of the novel, in sum, we have a picture of Anthony as a Hamlet-like figure—a melancholic, vacillating young man who displaces some of his self-disgust onto a melancholic female double. However, whereas Hamlet's anger toward his stepfather is justified, Anthony's anger toward Bloeckman is not. Without a true antagonist in his adulthood, Anthony would be free to attempt to recover from his unresolved feelings of abandonment. But throughout his life, he continues to believe Bloeckman, Gloria, and others wish to harm him, and he self-destructively clings to his belief in life's meaninglessness. Consequently, he regresses throughout his marriage. He becomes an "individual of bias and prejudice, with a longing to be emotionally undisturbed" (BD, 284).

During the war, he squanders an opportunity to redeem himself. One late chapter in the novel describes his time in boot camp in the South, where he is thrown in among people from various economic and ethnic strata. He responds well, for eventually "the system . . . grasp[s] him" (BD, 336), and he comes to separate people only by the categories of soldier and civilian. However, in other ways, he fails to progress, even regresses, during his time in the South. Instead of caring about those dying in the war, he maintains his defensive, ironical perspective upon death and mourning. He (like Gloria) finds a "melancholy pleasure" in reading newspaper accounts of men he knows among the casualties. Moreover, he has an affair with a Dorothy Raycroft, a woman for whom he does not care. Since he misses Gloria greatly, his affair promises him a way out of his long-dreaded fear of grief, an escape from the "devotion to Gloria that had been the chief jailer of his insufficiency" (BD, 325). However, Dorothy proves to be another uncanny double for Anthony, another person who embodies his inner

emotional nature, for she becomes obsessed with him. Her manipulative ploys cause him to break army rules and receive
punishment. Eventually he has a nervous breakdown, an unsurprising result in light of his lifelong efforts to repress emotion. When the war ends, he flees home to New York City
without telling Dorothy.

The culminating events of the novel complete his regression.
He takes up several occupations out of desperation—he and
Gloria move from apartment to apartment, each one in a
lower-class neighborhood than the last—but he soon fails in
every line of work. He has even less willpower to work than in
the past, partly because his drinking has developed into a severe case of alcoholism. Increasingly vitriolic in his bigotry, he
refers to his bank manager as a "greedy Mick" and shortly
after, in a drunken rage, he tracks down Bloeckman / Black
outside a nightclub and calls him a "Goddam Jew"—
"goddam," an ironic word in the context of Anthony's fate.
Bloeckman / Black cracks Anthony's jaw, blocks Anthony's
punch, and walks away with "conscious dignity," while some
nightclub workers throw Anthony into the gutter. Anthony's
incitement of conflict reminds us of his death wish against his
grandfather, for after his jaw is cracked, he mutters, "I'll kill
him" (BD, 437). Yet because of his alcoholic impairment and
his opponent's superior physical condition, the conflict seems
to result more from Anthony's self-destructiveness. In allowing himself to be abused, he is identifying with the aggressor,
submitting to the putative father. In another sign of that submission, when some sympathetic bystanders flag down a taxi
and ask him where he wants to be taken, Anthony leads them
to believe that he wishes to go to Tarrytown. We can conclude,
then, that he desires to return to the place where he once lived
with his abandoning parents and grandparents. He has combined his modernistic, Ulysses-like struggle to "go home
again" with his self-destructiveness.

At the end of the novel, as Gloria is in court learning that she
and Anthony will finally receive Grandfather Patch's inheritance, Anthony remains at home getting drunk. Then Dorothy
arrives, having finally tracked him down. He throws a chair at
her and says, "I'll kill you," as if desiring to kill off his emotional double. He then blacks out, and when Gloria and Dick

arrive at the apartment, Anthony resembles a "pert child," as he sorts through the stamp collection from his youth and shows no concern for others. In the final section of the novel, he is pushed around in a wheelchair by Gloria, and he remains out of touch with reality, speaking out loud to himself about his triumph over his hardships.

Readers have questioned why Fitzgerald seems to be rewarding Anthony by allowing him to receive the inheritance and remain convinced of his success in life, even if, as the title of the novel indicates, Anthony's afterlife will be less than blissful.[8] It seems more problematic that Fitzgerald suggests Gloria's failure to redeem herself. As two observers look upon the Patches at the end of the novel, one refers to Gloria as "unclean," an ironic echoing of Gloria's belief that those who have struggled in life are dirty. We might see Gloria as dirty not because she has experienced troubles, but because she is spiritually unclean, damned—she apparently stays with her husband only for his money. Though in wheeling around her enfeebled husband she has taken on the role of parental caretaker, we see that she does not truly care for him, since he reflects that everyone, including Gloria, eventually "turned against him." His view is probably accurate, for although he has a tenuous grip on reality at this point, we know that many people have severed their friendship with him, and we see that she does not speak to him at all in the final section.

Her fate seems undeserved, for her character has shown progress in the novel. Since Anthony's resistance to caring for the living and mourning the dead precipitates his fall, we would expect that Gloria's opposing behavior would be rewarded in the end. Both Anthony and Gloria show increased maturity in allowing themselves to fall in love with each other, but unlike Anthony, Gloria progresses beyond that point. At some point, Fitzgerald clearly considered tracing her development, for not long after Grandfather Patch stumbles upon the drunken revelry at their home, Gloria admits to the existence of "the skeleton, incomplete but nevertheless unmistakable, of her ancient abhorrence, a conscience" (BD, 278). Furthermore, in becoming a Bilphist after her parents' deaths, she demonstrates that she has fully embraced the importance of grief. Even if Fitzgerald, like his protagonist, felt her religion was a "soft" one, her belief in it still demonstrates progress over her youthful nihilism. Demonstrating further progression, she misses Anthony during his time in boot camp and forms the desire to have a child, to be a caregiver, when he returns. Though she is initially depicted as vampirish, he becomes the vampire eventually, for he serves as a "continual drain upon her moral strength" (BD, 371). It seems at first, then, that she will turn out to be a rare admirable female character in Fitzgerald's fiction.

Oddly, however, in the final two chapters of the novel, Fitzgerald abandons his delineation of her progression. He continues to depict her elitism but neglects her good qualities. After she becomes a Bilphist, we learn nothing about the role of the religion in her life. And after the war, Gloria suddenly has doubts about whether she ever wanted children, and she never broaches the subject to Anthony, though she is not one to avoid expressing her thoughts. Her development as a character is thus abruptly curtailed at the end of the novel, and Fitzgerald's final suggestion of her damnation does not accord with the direction of his narrative. Granted, *The Beautiful and Damned* is Anthony's story more so than hers, but we would expect Fitzgerald to depict her character with consistency, to reward her with redemption or at least to hint at the future possibility of it beyond the events of the novel. This problem may stem from forgetfulness on Fitzgerald's part, but it may also suggest that Fitzgerald ultimately shied away from endorsing Gloria's developing capacity for emotion. While we cannot know with certainty what Fitzgerald was thinking, we can at least see that his omniscient narrator shares Anthony's ambivalence toward the process of mourning. In discussing Mrs. Gilbert's death and funeral, the narrator states that the

> Bilphistic demiurge decided suddenly . . . that Mrs. Gilbert's soul had aged sufficiently in its present incarnation. In consequence Anthony took a miserable and hysterical Gloria out to Kansas City, where in the fashion of mankind, they paid the terrible and mind-shaking deference to the dead. (BD, 189)

The rigidly formal reference to Bilphistic reincarnation smacks of sarcasm, and the detached tone carries over into the description of the funeral, since it is referred to as the "fashion of mankind." Ultimately, then, portions of the novel undercut the social protest against cultural norms that characterizes the bulk of the work.

When Fitzgerald provides a criticism of his protagonist's story, "The Little Open Doors," his criticism could be applied to the ending of his own novel. In describing Anthony's stories, including this particular story of loss and the occult, Fitzgerald's narrator breaks from the stance of ironic detachment, calling them "wretched and pitiable," without a "spark of vitality" (BD, 302–303). Because all of Anthony's stories are rejected by magazine editors, Fitzgerald implies that popular magazine fiction has "vitality." In his career, Fitzgerald of course wrote fiction based on personal emotion that contained both commercial appeal and literary importance. When Anthony writes his story of loss for teary-eyed women, he might have produced well-written fiction by examining his own grief. Fitzgerald's inconsistent treatment of the issue of mourning in the novel indicates that he failed to heed his suggestion in this metafictional passage.

However, after finishing his next novel, *The Great Gatsby*, he would write, "All my harsh smartness has been kept ruthlessly out of it—it's the greatest weakness in my work, distracting and disfiguring it even when it calls up an isolated sardonic laugh."[9] Indeed, he would not "disfigure" his third novel as he did his second. Instead, he would provide a consistent validation of the importance of mourning.

5

Displaced Grief and Otherness in *The Great Gatsby*

> In *This Side of Paradise* (in a crude way) and in *Gatsby* I selected the stuff to fit a given mood or "hauntedness" or whatever you might call it."
>
> —*The Letters of F. Scott Fitzgerald*

A. B. PAULSON HAS NOTED THE PERVASIVE PRESENCE OF ORAL IMagery in *The Great Gatsby*, consisting of a "benign" oral theme and a "malign" one. For Paulson, both themes are united in Nick's image of the "fresh, clean breast of the New World,"[1] since that image embodies both promise and disappointment in the narrative. As an example of a purely benign image, Paulson alludes to a description of Gatsby's relationship with Daisy: Gatsby desires to "suck on the pap of life, gulp down the incomparable milk of wonder (GG, 86). Daisy, then, is objectified as the perfect mother. As one example of the malign oral imagery, Paulson refers to the moment when Myrtle's left breast is severed after she is fatally struck by Gatsby's car. Thus, after the idealized mother figure disappoints, another mother figure—Myrtle is a buxom, puppy-nurturer, as Paulson notes—is victimized. Paulson posits that the scene results from a "terrible infantile hostility from within Fitzgerald himself."[2]

If his mother's preoccupation with grief for his sisters sheds light on his hostility, then it becomes easier to comprehend the fact that in the novel, Fitzgerald satirically portrays various characters who experience chronic, underlying grief. I will argue that these characters displace their grief onto linking objects—Volkan's term for certain types of mementos, seen as bridges to the deceased, that serve a countertherapeutic role for the mourner. We recall that in contrast to other types of mementos, linking objects are those items that are often kept out of sight, and are valued on a largely unconscious level.[3] Louise's dolls, wrapped in tissue paper and preserved by Fitzgerald's mother, resembled linking objects, while Fitzgerald himself resembled a living linking object. Because linking objects serve as the chief signs of various characters' grief in *The Great Gatsby*, death has become commodified. Fitzgerald further suggests that while the old money members of society remain caught up in an underlying grief for their decline in society, those who are ethnic, racial, or economic outsiders, such as Gatsby, struggle to receive acceptance. Both the narrative's "primitive hostility" and its social critique reflect, in part, Fitzgerald's attitude toward his preoccupied, grieving mother.

Despite the mother-blaming impulse behind Fitzgerald's creativity, I will further argue that he also imbues the novel with a contradictory feminist implication. While both male and female characters fail to confront their grief, Fitzgerald implicitly blames a masculine-dominated world for fostering that repressiveness. Though Nick Carraway fears becoming effeminized by grief, as his oblique description of Myrtle's party suggests, he eventually validates the importance of mourning, turning his back on the extreme masculine world of the East. His evolving views result from his growing preference for Gatsby over the others he meets in the East. Gatsby grieves for Daisy as a child pines for the originary love object, and thus appears superior to the other characters who deny or displace the pain of loss. Previous critics have begun to address the issue of gender roles in the novel, though it would be difficult to infer a feminist implication in the novel from their observations.[4]

"HALTED" MOURNING

The Great Gatsby provides a more insightful, nuanced analysis of mourning behavior than Fitzgerald's previous two novels. Nick alludes to society's resistance to mourning in the opening of chapter 2, when he describes a Long Island landfill: "About half way between West Egg and New York the motor-road hastily joins the railroad and runs beside it for a quarter of a mile so as to shrink away from a certain desolate area of land. This is a valley of ashes" (GG, 21). Nick is implying that people "shrink" from thoughts of what ashes traditionally symbolize: decay, death, and mourning. We might say that characters in the novel wish to avoid thinking of the line from the nursery rhyme: "Ashes to ashes, we all fall down."

The depositing of ashes within this remote valley symbolizes a societal displacement of grief. Passersby cannot see the ashes, for within the valley, "ash-grey men swarm up with leaden spades and stir up an impenetrable cloud which screens their obscure operations from your sight" (GG, 21). The proximity of death hampers these men's will to live, for "with a transcendent effort . . . [they] move dimly and already crumbling through the powdery air" (GG, 21). However, train passengers eventually find themselves forced to confront the ashes, for Nick mentions that trains passing by must come to a "halt" in order to allow barges to travel under a drawbridge abutting the valley. Those on board "can stare at the dismal scene for as long as half an hour" (GG, 21). On a symbolic level, then, passengers remain suspended in a remote consideration of decay and death.[5]

Myrtle experiences a similar halting. She appears to select a dog collar as a linking object, for it bears some absurd connection in her mind with her deceased mother. She fleetingly referred to her mother when announcing to others her desire to purchase the collar and other items:

> I'm going to make a list of all the things I've got to get. A massage and a wave and a collar for the dog and one of those cute little ash trays where you touch a spring, and a wreath with a black silk bow for mother's grave that'll last all summer. (GG, 31)

Perhaps associating the circular motion of a massage and the circular "wave" of a hairdo with the exterior form of a collar, ash tray, wreath, and bow, Myrtle recalls her deceased mother only after thinking of various trivial needs. Though the collar is intended for the puppy housed in the Washington Heights apartment where she carries on her tryst with Tom Buchanan, perhaps its connection in her mind with her deceased mother encourages her to keep the collar out of sight, for she keeps it wrapped in tissue paper. We recall that Louise's dolls were wrapped in the same material. After Myrtle's death, the collar becomes a linking object for her husband, enabling him to avoid coping with his grief. When Michaelis attempts to console him, Wilson changes the subject, telling his friend to take the collar from a nearby drawer. Wilson then broods over the collar, gaining a dim understanding of Myrtle's adulterous life apart from him, but no longer thinking of her life *with* him.

Tom grieves in a similar way. Once a football star at Yale, he will "drift on forever seeking a little wistfully for the dramatic turbulence of some irrecoverable football game" (GG, 9)—seeking "linking phenomena," as Volkan would put it. The existence of such a chronic, underlying grief indicates his failure to confront his sense of loss. His inner grief helps to explain why his machismo is belied by a certain feminine nature, in Nick's view. Tom is "sturdy," "paternal," and "hulking," yet he walks in his riding clothes with an "effeminate swank" (GG, 9). He further demonstrates repressiveness after Myrtle's death. He says to Nick, "And if you think I didn't have my share of suffering—look here, when I went to give up that flat [in Washington Heights] and saw that damn box of dog biscuits sitting there on the sideboard I sat down and cried like a baby" (GG, 139). He does seem like a baby here, for his phrasing leads us to suspect that he externalized his grief, crying over the dog biscuits and possibly the apartment instead of Myrtle.

After Gatsby's death, Gatsby's father also turns to linking objects, demonstrating not so much a sadness over his son's death as an excitement over his son's mansion and other possessions. Meyer Wolfshiem follows suit, for he enjoys dining at the "old Metropole," since it is "[f]illed with faces dead and gone" (GG, 56). It thus serves as a linking phenomenon, a psychological meeting place for him and his deceased friends, including Rosy Rosenthal, who had his last meal there before he was fatally shot on the street outside. As Nick wonders why Wolfshiem suddenly leaves their table at the hotel, Gatsby says, "This is one of his sentimental days" (GG, 58). Thus, Wolfshiem is generally unsentimental and cannot confront pain for long before finding it necessary to flee from his emotions. The name of Wolfshiem's self-declared business, the Swastika

Holding Company, indicates his desire to move ahead in life—
swastikas were originally mystical symbols of spiritual renewal—while his avoidance of Gatsby's funeral suggests his
desire to move ahead without coming to terms with the past
first.

Because all these characters displace their grief onto an object or objects, death becomes commodified—a symptom of the
commodity-driven society Nick depicts throughout the novel.
We see more evidence of the attempted commodification of
death in Wolfshiem's cuff links of human molars, and by the
actions of Nick's ancestor, who paid someone to serve as a substitute in the Civil War while he stayed home to found a hard-
ware business.

THE RETURN OF THE REPRESSED "FEMININE" GRIEF

A bond salesman, Nick initially feels less uncomfortable
with the commodity-driven "man's world" than with "feminine" grief. We see his fear of "feminine" grief in his account
of Myrtle's party, an account that is appropriately placed at
the end of the chapter describing the male workers displacing
society's ashes into the landfill. Previous critics of the novel
have not pointed out the fact that Nick describes the party as
if it were a seance in which a deceased person produces a clan-
destine influence on the proceedings. That person, Myrtle's
mother, is the subject of an enormous photograph hanging on
the wall in the Washington Heights apartment, the most prominent object there. However, the photograph has been enlarged
to such an extent that the image of Myrtle's mother appears
blurry. Nick must stand at a distance in order to apprehend the
subject of the photograph. Metaphorically, then, the photograph resembles yet another linking object, its size representing its importance to Myrtle, yet its poor perceptibility
representing Myrtle's vague consciousness of her loss. In his
narrative, Nick pretends that the spirit of Myrtle's mother ultimately leads Myrtle to accept her filial obligation to mourn.
Appropriately, it is at the end of Myrtle's "seance" that she
suddenly thinks of her mother, albeit only in connection with
her shopping list.

When Nick identifies the subject of the photograph after his initial period of confusion, he notes that it "hover[s] like an ectoplasm on the wall" (GG, 26). He refers here not to the field of biology, but rather to the liquid-like substance that, according to those of a supernatural bent in the late nineteenth and early twentieth century, emanated from the spirits of the dead. Some felt that photographs could show evidence of the existence of ectoplasms. Many believers felt that ectoplasms produced telekinetic effects. Appropriately, Nick, who refers to himself as "enchanted" while he is at the party, suggests that some force other than the whiskey he has consumed controls his actions during the party: "I wanted to get out and walk eastward toward the park through the soft twilight but each time I tried to go I became entangled in some wild strident argument which pulled me back, as if with ropes, into my chair" (GG, 30). Meanwhile, a haze of cigarette smoke lingers in the air, Nick observes time passing with incomprehensible speed, and people and objects seem to teleport around the room, for people "disappear . . . [and] reappear," and Nick's hat ends up atop the chandelier.

When Jordan Baker mockingly suggests later in the novel that Tom hired a medium in order to uncover the source of Gatsby's wealth, she has accidentally come close to the truth, for while Tom does not know Gatsby during the time of Myrtle's party, he does encounter a "medium" there. Nick makes it appear as if, during the party, Myrtle achieves the entranced and levitated state to which the medium aspires: "Her laughter, her gestures, her assertions became more violently affected moment by moment and as she expanded the room grew smaller around her until she seemed to be revolving on a noisy, creaking pivot through the smoky air" (GG, 26–27). Nick suggests, then, that the ectoplasm of Myrtle's mother is emerging from the photograph and possessing her daughter.

If this interpretation seems far-fetched, it should be pointed out that Fitzgerald jestingly refers to a similar occurrence in "The Rich Boy" (1926). There, a character looks around for Arthur Conan Doyle when a smoke-filled room suggests to her the presence of an ectoplasm. Doyle was a noted believer in psychic phenomena, including ectoplasms. Myrtle's levitation also recalls other Fitzgerald fictional shenanigans, for one putatively comic scene in his unpublished first novel, *The Romantic Egotist*, involves a levitating carpet. It should be further pointed out that Nick's *prosopopeic* use of the photograph—his representation of an absent person who appears to have the ability to take action—accords with the structure and style of his narrative. Like the photograph, the billboard of Doctor T.J. Eckleburg influences Wilson's thoughts. Other parts of the text show Nick's favoring of personification, a literary device closely related to *prosopopeia*, as in his description of the "running, jumping lawn" outside the Buchanan's home and the "fresh, green breast" of the Dutch settlers' New World.

In addition, the gender implications of Nick's account recall a part of the cultural "work" of seances in real life. Not only have seances long served to comfort those in grief, but in the modern spiritualist movement, which began in the mid-nineteenth century, mediumship was traditionally a female role, enabling women to transgress constraints placed upon their behavior, as R. Laurence Moore has recently explained. Mediums, Moore notes, insisted that the spirits ordered them to drink whiskey, take sexual liberties, and to leave their husbands.[6] Since the medium's supernatural energy was said to include a sexual energy, the female medium's role was a further threat to the norm. Nick's account of the party parallels all of these aspects of seances, for not only does it include whiskey, but the women control conversations, discussing Myrtle's affair, as well as the possibility of her divorcing George and Tom divorcing Daisy. And as the seeming medium, Myrtle embodies the sexuality associated with her role, for Nick previously adverted to Myrtle's "sensuous" and "smouldering" nature. Moreover, before the party, she had slipped into another room of the apartment to couple with Tom, while Nick read a racy novel of hers in the main room of the apartment.[7] In a further similarity to seances, the males in the room experience a draining of energy, an experience reminiscent of the many published accounts in which sitters professed that the medium had drained power from their bodies, particularly their legs. Nick cannot move from his chair—loses control of his legs, in effect—Tom for once appears inconspicuous for an extended stretch of time, while Mr. McKee falls into a drunken stupor.

The male characters' inability to move suggests a symbolic castration, but Tom responds when he suddenly breaks Myrtle's nose, another symbolic castration that puts the empowered medium back into her accustomed place. Unlike Tom, however, both Nick and McKee become more "effeminate" by the end of the party. While Nick describes McKee as a "pale, feminine man" when he first meets him, it is only by its conclusion that McKee's atypical masculinity emerges fully. McKee becomes enmeshed with Nick in a homoerotic charade. In detailing the homoerotic subtext, Keath Fraser has noted that Nick wipes some shaving cream from McKee's face, while shortly after, Nick and McKee descend in the building's elevator toward McKee's apartment, whereupon the elevator boy says, "Keep your hands off the lever" (GG, 32). Moreover, Fraser notes, Nick interrupts his narrative for some reason, then mentions suddenly that he is standing beside Mr. McKee's bed who lies in it while clad only in underwear. Afterward, Nick waits in "the cold lower level" of Pennsylvania station.[8]

Rather than jumping to the conclusion that Nick has had a homosexual experience or fantasy involving McKee, and that he is a believer in telekinesis, it is more reasonable to conclude that his subtextual plots serve as his sheepish confession of a personal fear: that he feels unmanned by displays of grief. In a classic case of the return of the repressed, Myrtle's mother, a symbol of the nineteenth-century matriarch overthrown by the masculine destructiveness of the Great War, has suddenly returned with sudden force. Nick pretends that she has foisted nineteenth-century sentimentality—"feminine" grief—onto him. As Wolfshiem suddenly flees from the Metropole after a spell of sentimentality, Nick has desired to flee from the apartment building rather than remain "halted" there, as if by the side of the valley of ashes. At this point in his life, he is more comfortable with "masculine" repressiveness.

DAISY'S MATERNAL GRIEF

In portraying Myrtle's party as a seance, Nick provides a parallel to his portrayal of Daisy's behavior. Much as Myrtle becomes consumed with her "seance" and neglects her new puppy, Daisy is consumed with a mysterious sense of grief and resists her maternal role. Though she likes to pretend "she had done gay, exciting things just a while since and that there were gay, exciting things hovering in the next hour" (GG, 11), her grief appears to reside permanently at the borders of her consciousness. Her condition first becomes evident in the opening chapter of the novel, after Nick hyperbolically informs her that since she moved from Chicago, "[a]ll the cars [there] have the left rear wheel painted black as a mourning wreath and there's a persistent wail all night along the North Shore" (GG, 11). She responds with a sudden gush of feeling—"How gorgeous! Let's go back, Tom. Tomorrow!" (GG, 11). Misery loves company. Repeatedly in the opening chapter, Nick mentions her "sad" face, and he later observes her "aching grieving beauty." Daisy displays the existential angst commonly found in those in mourning: "What'll we plan?" she says. "What do people plan?" (GG, 13). Her grief becomes further apparent when she suspects that she has spotted a nightingale, that symbol of human mortality in Keats and elsewhere, outside her home.

Interestingly, immediately after she expresses her desire to see the mourning wreaths allegedly on the automobiles of Chicago, Daisy says to Nick, "You ought to see the baby" (GG, 11). Though he feels she has made this remark "irrelevantly," he learns it is not a non sequitur, for the birth of her daughter Pammy illuminates the nature of her mysterious grief. Pammy might at first seem to play only a minor role in Daisy's life (and thus in any interpretation of the novel), since Daisy spends hardly any time with her. However, Daisy's neglect results not from a lack of concern for Pammy but rather, from a severe, half-hidden parental anxiety. We see this anxiety later in the chapter, after Tom upsets Daisy by speaking to Myrtle on the phone. When Nick perceives her distress, he inquires about her daughter in the belief that the subject will make her feel less upset. However, thoughts of Pammy make Daisy feel worse, as becomes apparent when she then describes the events occurring just after her daughter's birth:

> Well, she was less than an hour old and Tom was God knows where. I woke up out of the ether with an utterly abandoned feeling and asked the nurse right away if it was a boy or a girl. She

told me it was a girl, and so I turned my head away and wept. "All right," I said, "I'm glad it's a girl. And I hope she'll be a fool— that's the best thing a girl can be in this world, a beautiful little fool." (GG, 17)[9]

Daisy feels that acting like a child, like a "little fool," must serve as the highest ambition of a woman in her society. The vendor who sells Myrtle a puppy would understand Daisy's sense of confinement, for he pretends the puppy is a male, not a "bitch," as if he knows that males are worth more in his society. Appropriately, he resembles John D. Rockefeller, that icon of commodity-driven culture. Daisy has displaced her grief over her social role onto her daughter. Like Daisy, the two women, or "stage 'twins,' " at Gatsby's party seem to grieve for their girlhood, for they perform a "baby act in costume" (GG, 39). Pammy's fate as a "little fool" means that she has been socially stillborn, a fate symbolized in her single, fleeting appearance in the novel. There, she enters the room and Daisy says to her, "Did mother get powder on your old yellowy hair?" (GG, 91). The powder on her "old" hair represents a sudden, grotesque aging, much as the dust that gathers on other characters' bodies represents their mortality.

Though Daisy's discussion of her daughter's birth seems to touch upon a serious problem in her life, Nick eventually decides that a "basic insincerity" underlies her words, and he observes a smirk emerging on her face. However, as her account of her time in the maternity ward is moving, it must reflect true emotion. Indeed, Nick's reaction and Daisy's smirk come only after she diffuses the subject of discussion by generalizing: "You see I think everything's terrible anyhow" (GG, 17), she says, paving her emotion with homily then capping it with unconvincing and boastful cynicism. She surrenders to her grief-repressing, male-dominated society.

Gatsby's Relationship(s) with the Preoccupied Parent

After Myrtle's death, Michaelis says to Wilson, "Ever had any children?. . . Did you ever have any children" (GG, 122)? Michaelis thus realizes that parents turn to their children in order to cope with loss. In his relationship with Daisy, Gatsby resembles a consolatory child. In fact, he resembles a living linking object, since his presence will allow her to return to a time of past happiness, or so he believes. A man of "appalling sentimentality," Gatsby feels he can magically "fix everything just the way it was before" (GG, 86). He disagrees with Nick's assertion that "you can't repeat the past" (GG, 86).

In serving as a living linking object for her "stillborn" baby, Gatsby undergoes a symbolic rebirth. Upon first gaining an awareness of Gatsby's desire for Daisy, Nick says, "He came alive to me, delivered suddenly from the womb of his purpose-less splendor" (GG, 62). As a living linking object, Gatsby's oral view of Daisy takes on added meaning: he seeks "a secret place above the trees—he could climb to it, *if he climbed alone,* and once there he could suck on the pap of life, gulp down the incomparable milk of wonder (GG, 86; emphasis mine). The conditional clause "if he climbed alone" suggests that Gatsby can receive nourishment from Daisy only if she does not con-tinue to remain preoccupied with someone else. However, as she seems distracted by her grief over her sense of confinement and Pammy's spiritual stillbirth, she is emotionally unavail-able. She describes herself as "p-paralyzed with happiness" when she first speaks in the novel, yet it appears more as if she is paralyzed with grief.

Hence, we can gain a better understanding of Gatsby's shock when he finally meets Pammy. He stands and stares, as if ap-prehending a ghost. Nick says of Gatsby's reaction, "I don't think he had ever really believed in its existence before" (GG, 91). Her haunting appearance in this scene signals the begin-ning of the end of Gatsby's relationship with Daisy, as if she serves as proof that Daisy is in fact preoccupied.[10] Gatsby has shown great poise in vying with Tom for Daisy's love, but Pammy serves as his more unnerving antagonist at this point. After Gatsby feels shocked by her presence, his poise begins to crumble, and Daisy soon displays her inability to relinquish her grief and commit herself to him. He will not be reborn as the new child who will "fix" her sense of loss. When Tom and Gatsby argue over Daisy in the climactic scene of the novel, Tom denigrates Gatsby by referring to him as if he were aban-doned at birth. Tom pronounces Gatsby "Mr. Nobody from

Nowhere" (GG, 101), and tells him, Daisy "didn't know you were alive" in the past (GG, 103). The history of Gatsby's mansion has already portended his eventual failure to regain her. Although the original owner built it with a desire to "Found a Family," his children, as if anxious to forget about him, sold the house shortly after his death, a mourning wreath still on the door. Thus, others' frozen grief mocks the ambitions of both the original and current owner of the mansion.

Gatsby's desire for Daisy serves as an example of "true" grief in the novel, the counterpoint to the behavior of the other characters Nick meets in the East, and the counterpoint to Nick's college classmates, whose "secret griefs" were "usually plagiaristic and marred by obvious suppressions" (GG, 5). While the determination to repeat the past is not a mature response to loss, Gatsby at least confronts his inner grief, thus appearing "less infantile" than other characters in the novel who do not. For a character in this novel or in many other canonical works of American literature to appear "less infantile" than others is for a character to appear surprisingly mature. Gatsby grieves in his first appearance in the novel, stretching out his arms and gazing across the Long Island Sound toward the green light at the end of Daisy's dock. Unlike Wolfshiem and other characters, Gatsby does not have his "sentimental days"; he is always prepared to grieve. Though Nick initially feels that Gatsby displays "appalling sentimentality," much as he is put off by Myrtle's "seance", his growing admiration for Gatsby helps him to validate the importance of mourning.

BIRTH, DEATH, AND OTHERNESS

In coming to identify with Gatsby, Nick increasingly turns against those who do not grieve "properly." His reversal is bound up with ethnic, racial, and class implications, for those who do not grieve "properly" are the social insiders. Racial difference came into Fitzgerald's focus briefly in a scene from *The Beautiful and Damned*. There, we recall, the previous janitor in Anthony's apartment building, a white man, dies from pneumonia and is replaced by a black man, occurrences that disturb the bigoted Anthony. *Tender Is the Night* involves another peculiar scenario, which we learn about just after Nicole's thoughts flash back to the time when she experienced a schizophrenic fear after her second child's birth. Nicole hallucinated that her child was black, and as if the child's identity were permanently marked by her mother's paranoia, she was given the name of Topsy, a stereotypical name for a black person, as in *Uncle Tom's Cabin*. Fitzgerald knew this novel,[11] and he clearly took an interest in stereotypical names for black people, since one of his notebooks contains a list of them. In effect, in *The Beautiful and Damned* and *Tender Is the Night*, the condition of racial otherness is linked with the experience of entering a new world and confronting ambivalence from those fraught with anxiety. Gatsby similarly meets maternal ambivalence after his "rebirth." Since these situations recall the circumstances of Fitzgerald's birth, an element of self-ambivalence may underlie the author's depiction of difference, as I first suggested in chapter 1. Accordingly, throughout *The Great Gatsby*, Nick has an ambivalent attitude toward minorities, displaying both condescension and empathy, as in his attitude toward Gatsby.

While Daisy grieves for her "*white* girlhood" (GG, 19; emphasis mine), Gatsby has come to make himself "more white." He has acquired the wealth of an aristocrat, after allying himself with another outsider, the Jewish Wolfshiem, and has anglicized his name from Jimmy Gatz. From the beginning of his relationship with Gatsby, Nick finds Gatsby's parvenu appearance important. Shortly after meeting Gatsby, Nick "would have accepted without question the information that Gatsby sprang from the swamps of Louisiana or from the Lower East Side of New York" (GG, 41). In the novel's opening, Nick has "snobbishly" admitted to his elitism: "a sense of the fundamental decencies is parcelled out unequally *at birth*" (GG, 5; emphasis mine). This image evokes Nicole's ambivalence to Topsy's birth, and Daisy's to Gatsby's "rebirth."

Allusions to birth and otherness abound in the novel. In his reaction to Tom's discussion of Goddard's racist theories in *The Rise of the Colored Empires*, Nick further shows his ambivalence toward those who are "born" into a world of difference. Tom's concern with the alleged decline of the white race serves as the cultural counterpart to his underlying grief for the gridirons of his college days. Goddard's book is a fictional version of *The Rising Tide of Color against White World Supremacy* (1920), in which Lothrop Stoddard argues that the world's population consists of five major races—black, brown, red, yellow, and white—the last of which would eventually be dominated by the others unless preventative (reactionary) measures were taken. As Stoddard's tract was widely read and discussed in Fitzgerald's time, many readers of *The Great Gatsby* in the 1920s would have recognized the allusion to Stoddard's theories and would likely have been aware of the fact that the birth rates of each race were of central importance to his argument. Stoddard finds cause for alarm in the declining birth rates among whites and the rising rates among other races. Moreover, Stoddard is also profoundly troubled by the Great War, his reaction to it largely based upon his concern with the intraracial nature of the conflict, furthering the decline of the white population.

Though Nick does not share Tom's outrage over Goddard's theories, his narrative does demonstrate concern over birth and death trends and social otherness, as we see in his account of East and West Egg. Since eggs of course are symbols of birth, we might say that those taking up residence in West Egg are born into their roles as social upstarts. Like Gatsby, they are confronting others in a state of grief, for as Nick implies through his list of people attending Gatsby's parties, the East Eggers are a dying class: Doctor Webster Civet drowned the summer before, Edgar Beever's hair, like Pammy's powdered, "old" hair, "turned cotton-white one winter afternoon for no good reason at all" (GG, 49), and S. B. Whitebait is "well over sixty." The inhabitants of West Egg, in contrast, appear closer to the bloom of youth, as symbolized by the flowery names among their set: Newton Orchid and Ernest Lilly. Thus, as Gatsby must contend with the problem of Daisy's sense of loss, the "newborn" West Eggers must struggle for acceptance from the East Eggers, whose fortunes are on the wane. In remaining aloof during Gatsby's parties, Nick shows his reluctance to accept such a changing society.

In Nick's narrative, the poorest members of society appear to be experiencing rapid increases in birth rates. Since Daisy still grieves over the birth of her first child, and since she and Tom have separate bedrooms (there is a reference to Daisy's pink bedroom), there is little possibility that this family of old money will have additional children. In contrast, Myrtle, a member of the lower class, strongly desires to procreate, for she married Wilson because she mistakenly "thought he knew something about breeding" (GG, 30). Now, perhaps, she feels that Tom will be of use to her for this end, though—no doubt to his relief—he has so far proved himself ineffective. A couplet in a song sung by Gatsby's boarder, Klipspringer, suggests that other members of the lower class have achieved what Myrtle desires. Klipspringer sings, "One thing's sure and nothing's surer / The rich get richer and the poor get—children" (GG, 75).

Moreover, as Stoddard refers to increasing birth rates among nonwhite races, the imagery of one passage of the novel, in which Nick travels in Gatsby's car over the Queensboro Bridge, suggests Nick's ambivalence toward this trend among blacks:

> Over the great bridge, with the sunlight through the girders making a constant flicker upon the moving cars . . . The city seen from the Queensboro Bridge is always the city seen for the first time, in its first wild promise of all the mystery and the beauty in the world.
>
> A dead man passed us in a hearse heaped with blooms, followed by two carriages with drawn blinds and by more cheerful carriages for friends. The friends looked out at us with the tragic eyes and short upper lips of south-eastern Europe . . . As we crossed Blackwells Island a limousine passed us, driven by a white chauffeur, in which sat three modish Negroes, two bucks and a girl. I laughed aloud as the yolks of their eyeballs rolled toward us in haughty rivalry. (GG, 54–55)

Many of the elements of this scene—the passage through a bridge, the bridge's feminine name, the surrounding water and daylight, the emphasis upon the firstness of the moment, the "yolks" of the black passengers' eyes—suggest a moment of birth. In effect, the birth or rebirth of the black race occurs simultaneously with the death of the white race, specifically the Eastern European segment of it, the segment at the center of the Great War. It seems that, like Gatsby in his relationship with Daisy, the blacks in the limousine are born into a world not only of grief, but of conflicted grief, for a hint of repressiveness exists in some of the whites' behavior. Despite their "tragic" eyes, those further back in the funeral procession travel in "more cheerful" carriages. Thus, the whites' acceptance of a changing world, one in which, as this passage of the text suggests, they are dying out while the black race remains productive, would be made all the more difficult.

Nick's derogatory language and sarcastic laughter here indicate again that he does not differ so much from Tom. He is only more discreet in his bigotry. Eventually, however, he overcomes his ambivalence toward Gatsby's parvenu status. In a previous manuscript version of the novel, Nick refers to Gatsby admiringly as "someone from a race yet unborn," as if he has come to see Gatsby as transcending the problem of hereditary difference. In the final version, Nick comes to the conclusion that Gatsby is "worth the whole damn bunch [of bluebloods] put together" (120). Moreover, Nick eventually redirects the brunt of his snobbishness, for instead of looking down upon minorities born into a world of mourning, he comes to stress his distance from those who cannot confront their grief. We see his new focus in a passage of the text in which he observes the reactions of Wilson and Tom to the knowledge of their wives' infidelity:

> [George] had discovered that Myrtle had some sort of life apart from him in another world and the shock had made him physically sick. I stared at him and then at Tom, who had made a parallel discovery less than an hour before—and *it occurred to me that there was no difference between men, in intelligence or race, so profound as the difference between the sick and the well.* Wilson was so sick that he looked guilty, unforgivably guilty—as if he had just got some poor girl with child. (GG, 96–97; emphasis mine)

Thus, while Nick demonstrates a continuing belief that racial difference remains significant, his sense of Wilson and Tom's peculiar appearance leads him to believe that there is a more "profound" type of difference. But what is that type of difference—what does he mean exactly by the "sick" and the "well"? Wilson's sickness takes the form of "shock"; he is nearly immobilized by his emotional pain and struggles to attend to his du-

ties at his gas station. More specifically, Wilson, like Tom, is
shocked by the emotion of grief, a feeling that his wife is estranged from him, "in another world." These characters, unable to work through their sense of bereavement, have become
cut off from the everyday world. They resemble the workers in
the valley of ashes whose "obscure operations" can hardly be
seen by the train and automobile passengers, who are eager to
shrink from the valley.

When Myrtle is killed, Wilson's sense of shock intensifies and
leads him toward an extreme reaction, furthering Nick's belief
in the peculiarity of those unable to grieve. In fatally shooting
Gatsby and then shooting himself, he is "reduced [in newspaper accounts] to a man "deranged by grief" (GG, 127). Though
reductive, the public perception is essentially correct, for Wilson's shock causes his acts of violence. He wanders from the
valley of ashes as if to wander from his grief, and his bottled-
up emotions return suddenly in both homicidal and suicidal
form. Ironically, he seems more human than some of the other
characters, for his squeezes of the trigger, actions guided by
unbridled emotion, stand apart from the artificial gestures of
other characters. Thus, it becomes clear why Nick refers in the
beginning of the novel to the "foul dust [that] floated in the
wake of [Gatsby's] dreams" (GG, 6), for Wilson has tracked
that dust from the valley into Gatsby's life. In truth, however,
the dust and ashes of grief in Daisy's life have already brought
an end to Gatsby's dreams.

In attending to Gatsby's funeral and in relating his experiences in the East, Nick shows he has learned from Gatsby
about the importance of confronting the dust and ashes. He
sees that we are "borne back ceaselessly into the past" (GG,
141)—that there is no way to avoid bereavement. His narrative
is, after all, an elegiac tribute to his deceased friend, allowing
him to resist his society's gender roles and undergo the process
of mourning. Consequently, he is able to accept his ambivalence toward the object of his mourning. He feels that Gatsby
"represented everything [flashiness] for which [he has] unaf-
fected scorn," and at the same time, he recognizes Gatsby's
"extraordinary gift for hope, [his] romantic readiness" (GG, 6).
In confronting his sense of loss, he stands above those in the

East, who experience only brief bursts of "feminine" grief, remaining otherwise distanced from their sense of loss, halted by the side of the valley of ashes that exists in the center of their world and eventually levels the dreams of insiders and outsiders alike.

6

"The Last Hope of a Decaying Clan": A Case of Male Hysteria in *Tender Is the Night*

> Thou wast not born for death, immortal Bird! No hungry
> generations tread thee down . . .
> > —Keats, "Ode to a Nightingale"

> Receding from a grief, it seems necessary to retrace the
> same steps that brought us there.
> > —narrator in *Tender Is the Night*

ITS PROTAGONIST AND ITS LEADING LADY A PSYCHIATRIST AND HIS patient respectively, *Tender Is the Night* invites discussion about the issue of transference love in the novel. Do feelings applicable toward people from the past inform Dick and Nicole's emotions and behavior in their present relationship? Addressing Dick's countertransference, Jeffrey Berman has noted that Dick's "rescue fantasy," his infantile "desire to love so intensely as to both engulf and be engulfed," underlies his repetition of the incestuous relationship between Nicole and her father.[1] This chapter will locate Dick's incestuous countertransference within his overwhelming desire to rescue others in mourning, a desire fostered by the deaths of his two sisters. Previous critics have not explored in detail the importance of these tragedies in Dick's life. Sharing his protagonist's experience with sibling loss, Fitzgerald becomes caught up in Dick's fantasy, portraying Nicole as someone caught between a fear of loss and a denial of that fear—a conflict suggesting a split in the ego, but one very different from the schizophrenia supposedly plaguing her. Examining the novel in this light, we can better understand her mysterious recovery at the end of the novel, and better appreciate Dick's tragic flaws—aspects of the novel that readers have consistently questioned.

Volkan's theory of the living linking object, the person who serves as an emblematic meeting ground between the mourner and the deceased, will be useful to our discussion of Dick's conflict. Whereas Nick's narrative provides a hint of Gatsby's role as linking object in *The Great Gatsby*, *Tender Is the Night* provides a more detailed perspective on the role. To further our insight into Dick's conflicted nature, it will be necessary to recall the struggle the living linking object experiences in attempting to integrate his or her self-image with both the mourner's self-image and the parent's image of the deceased, a process that can promote a creative adaptation but, if unsuccessful, a splitting of the ego.[2]

Such a split in Dick's ego resembles Nicole's struggle over loss. It also loosely resembles shell shock, a malady Fitzgerald alludes to in the novel as well. Though as Berman has observed, Fitzgerald demonstrates a lack of understanding of basic psychoanalytic terminology, the complexities of schizophrenia, and the "theoretical and clinical intricacies of transference love," Fitzgerald's focus on the issue of shell shock, an important phenomenon of early-twentieth-century society that demonstrates his insight into the gender dynamics of his time.[3] Elaine Showalter has discussed shell shock's similarity to hysteria, the "female malady." While women in the nineteenth century suffering from hysteria were internalizing their protest against normative gender roles, men suffering from shell shock during and after the Great War were wracked with emotions that they, following their culture's taboo on masculine emotion, had attempted to repress. Shell shock contained similar symptoms to hysteria, such as nervousness, grief, and paralysis. The depression and fatigue of many shell shocks also recalled symptoms of neurasthenia, another "female malady." Showalter further discusses shell shock as a response to a "whole range of male social obligations" outside of the military.[4]

Dick never saw action in the war, but he does struggle to cope with social obligations outside the military. His desire to empathize with others' grief, to share its burden, conflicts with his role as a male in society. Consequently, he represses his "unmanly" nature with increasing intensity over the course of his life. In a case of the return of the repressed, his repressed emotion only increases his desire to empathize. He then attempts in sudden piques of desperation to rescue others from their sense of loss, even while putting his career and marriage in jeopardy. Ultimately, his conflicting desires lead to a condition very much like hysteria / shell shock.

CLINGING WOMEN AND WITHDRAWN MEN

An exchange between Nicole and Abe North illuminates the distinction in the novel between masculine and feminine behavior. Nicole states, "I am a woman and my business is to hold things together," while Abe responds, "My business is to tear them apart."[5] Thus, according to Nicole and Abe, women draw closer to others in response to a disruptive influence, while men tend to revel in loss, aggravating its wound. This distinction applies to Baby Warren's character. When Dick asks her why she remains unmarried, she implies that she is still consumed with grief for the two men she has loved, one who died in the war, and another who broke off the relationship. Having admired the "formality" of these Englishmen, she now allows herself to be courted only by other Englishmen, as if she is searching for linking objects. Thus, she is "femininely" drawn toward others in reaction to loss. Since she remains single, her new boyfriends apparently fail to measure up to the first two. Consequently, her grief remains unresolved, for she "relish[es] the foretaste of death, prefigured by the catastrophe of friends" (TITN, 171). In remaining single, she is unsympathetically portrayed as unfeminine: "wooden and onanistic," "alien from touch." She resembles her "grandfather, cool and experimental" (TITN, 175), displaying a facility for financial matters instead of interpersonal relationships. Thus, she ultimately responds "masculinely" to grief.

The McKiscos' experience of losing a child also illuminates the novel's distinction between the feminine and masculine reaction to loss. Explaining why he feels a need to fight in a duel with Tommy Barban, Albert McKisco says of his wife Violet:

She's very hard when she gets an advantage over you. We've been married twelve years, we had a little girl seven years old and she died and after that you know how it is. We both played around on the side a little, nothing serious but drifting apart—she called me a coward out there tonight. (TITN, 45)

The death of their daughter gave him a sense of powerlessness and Violet took "advantage," viewing him as unmanly, a "coward." Meanwhile, she assumed a "masculine" role, for she acted "hard." And like him, she "drifted" from the relationship, aggravating the familial wound. McKisco implies, then, that his loss of relative power has led him to pursue the extreme masculinity of fighting in the duel, as if to transcend anxiety. However, he gets drunk before the duel, and he stands so far away from Barban during the duel that Barban, an experienced combatant, does not wound him. Still, McKisco becomes secure about his manliness again in surviving the duel. He eventually becomes a best-selling author, "his success . . . founded psychologically upon his duel with Tommy Barban, upon the basis of which, as it withered in his memory, he had created, afresh, a new self-respect" (TITN, 206). Though we might find the situation psychologically implausible, he has regained a sense of power over his wife, not by working through his "unmanning" grief for his daughter, but by convincing himself of his imperviousness to pain.

Luis Campion serves in the novel as an example of a male who demonstrates "feminine" grief. At Dick's party, he shows a "blatant effeminacy" and a "disinterested motherliness" (TITN, 33), as he indiscriminately concerns himself with whomever is near him at the table. Later, when he awaits the duel between Tommy Barban and Albert McKisco, his "femininity" becomes exaggerated. He empathizes so strongly with the participants in the duel that he forgets he is not experiencing their crisis. He "sigh[s] suddenly thinking of his own griefs. 'I almost wish it were I. I might as well be killed now I have nothing to live for' " (TITN, 41). He nervously grabs Rosemary Hoyt's arm without invitation, and she asks him to let go. However, his suffering has already shown itself to be bathetic, for he has brought along a movie camera to the duel, as if out of a desire to make the sort of contrived Hollywood movie in which Rosemary acts. He has stated, "But now I don't care—I wash my hands of [the affair] completely" (TITN, 48). The narrator indicates that Rosemary thinks of Campion as "dehumanized" when she sees his movie camera. His grief has become so overwrought that he no longer seems to appreciate the potential loss of human life.

Barban acts so "masculinely" that he loses his humanity as well. Tommy Barb(ari)an flouts the need for human contact, exiling himself from society for extended periods of time and serving as a mercenary. He fights with little concern for the cause involved. He has only a vague fear of inanimate object loss, for he mentions that he has fought the Communists because they might one day seize his "property." The violence of war temporarily inoculates him against the pain of grief, since, as he prepares to go to another war in the first book of the novel, he appears to be under a "special stimulus." Accordingly, he implies that he does not have any strong ties to the world, any deep fear of loss: "I have no home" (TITN, 29). Further alluding to his repulsion for emotional bonds, he states, "When I'm in a rut, I come to see the Divers, because then I know that in a few weeks I'll want to go to war" (TITN, 29).

Abe North's personality veers toward a similar extreme "masculinity." He suffers from depression, feels "tired of women's worlds" (81), and resists his wife's attempts to help him. A professional composer, he used to spend hours "making love" to the piano, that icon of nineteenth century "feminine" domesticity, but his "survivant will, once a will to live, [has] now become a will to die" (TITN, 82). Despite his desire to leave the world he once cherished, he also feels strongly drawn toward his past, for his alcoholism medicates against an inner sense of loss. When he is drunk, he is "happy to live in the past. The drink [makes] past happy things contemporary with the present, as if they were still going on, contemporary even with the future as if they were about to begin again" (TITN, 103). Ultimately, he exits the harmonious "feminine" world when he dies in a bar fight. Appropriately, Barban, as someone routinely exposed to the "masculine" world of violent disharmony, is the one to pass on the news of Abe's death to Dick.

Fitzgerald also focuses on the issue of loss in his portrayal of Nicole's familial background. In outlining his family's history,

Mr. Warren, Nicole's father, mentions that "there was a boy that died" (TITN, 125).[6] His grief for his son appears to have drawn him closer to Nicole, for he refers to the death at the same time that he implies she was his favorite child. In doting upon her, he thus entered further into the "feminine" domestic world. The trend continued in the aftermath of another death in the family. He mentions that he became "father and mother both" (TITN, 124) to Nicole upon his wife's death. He elaborates, "After her mother died when she was little she used to come into my bed every morning, sometimes she'd sleep in my bed. I was sorry for the little thing" (TITN, 127–28). Tragically, by committing incest with her, he failed to tame his "masculine" destructiveness in assuming a "feminine" role.

Her resultant schizophrenia shackles her "feminine" nature. Mr. Warren states that she "seemed to freeze up" (TITN, 128) after he abused her, a reaction that carries over in her "masculine" tendency as an adult to remain self-absorbed. However, in her transference toward Dick, her "feminine" inclination to seek emotional support reveals itself. In a letter to him, she expresses her sense of loss: "My family have shamefully neglected me, there's no use asking them for help or pity" (TITN, 121). Dick states that he is "only a sort of stuffed figure" (TITN, 130) to Nicole, and indeed he is. She hardly knows Dick when she begins writing her intimate letters to him, but this situation is not an obstacle in a relationship in which transference creates the love. As she once looked to her father to help her through her experience of maternal loss, to be "father and mother both," her image of Dick seems "stuffed" with her image of her mother. She fears his masculinity, a manifestation of her unconscious memory of abuse, but she is attracted to his "feminine" side. She writes to him, "I have only gotten to like boys who are rather sissies" (TITN, 120), and she appreciates the "feminine" empathy he shows as a psychiatrist:

That part of him which seemed to fit his reddish Irish coloring she knew least; she was afraid of it, yet more anxious to explore—this was his more masculine side: the other part, the trained part, the consideration in the polite eyes, she expropriated without question, as most women did. (TITN, 141)

Having lost her parents, she worries about losing Dick. She imagines that he will die in combat, telling him in a letter, "you are far away, perhaps killed" (TITN, 120). Her mother died after a protracted illness, and now when Dick delays in writing back to her, she responds in a letter, "I keep thinking at night you have been sick" (TITN, 123). The night is not tender for her; it is a time of loss. He indirectly admits late in the novel that he has replaced her father who attempted to replace her mother. When he exits an Italian courtroom after being tried for assaulting a member of the carabinieri, he responds to a crowd of people outside who have mistaken him for a recently arrested child rapist and murderer: "I want to explain to these people how I raped a five-year-old girl. Maybe I did" (TITN, 236). And late in the novel comes further evidence of Dick's maternal role in Nicole's life. The narrator refers to Nicole's "dry suckling at his lean chest" (TITN, 276).

Bereavement serves a particularly important role in our understanding of the Speers family as well. Despite the fact that Mrs. Speers remains in good health, she readily awaits her death. She is "fresh in appearance but she [is] tired; death beds make people tired indeed" (TITN, 23). Her feelings have undoubtedly been encouraged by her experience as a survivor of two husbands. She further responds to her grief by envisioning her daughter Rosemary as a linking object: "One of her husbands had been a cavalry officer and one an army doctor, and they both left something to her that she tried to present intact to Rosemary. By not sparing Rosemary she made her hard" (TITN, 11). Thus, Mrs. Speers sees herself and her daughter as appropriating the "masculine" nature of her husbands. She feels that Rosemary, "for all her delicate surface, [is] a young mustang, perceptibly by Captain Doctor Hoyt, U. S. A." (TITN, 164).

In balancing their "masculine" and "feminine" grief, rather than subsuming one mode of behavior to the other as Mr. Warren did, Mrs. Speers and her daughter demonstrate a better method of working through the pain of loss than other characters. Mrs. Speers displays "feminine" behavior in drawing closer to her daughter in reaction to loss, and she also displays "masculine" rigidity, a "cheerful stoicism," apparently what her husbands left "intact" to her. This amalgam of traits helps her to cope with loss, for while she suffers from chronic grief, she has weathered the two tragedies in her life better than other characters have weathered theirs. Her balanced nature also helps keep in check the influence of her unresolved grief upon Rosemary. Though she fears for her daughter's health, likely another reaction to her losses, she has tempered that fear so that it does not hinder Rosemary's willingness to take necessary chances in life. In fact, Mrs. Speers's parental concern only allows her to be prepared when illness occurs. When Rosemary needed to dive repeatedly into a Venice canal the previous January for the filming of a movie, Mrs. Speers waited on the set with a doctor (Mr. Speers's profession) ready, a precaution that proved useful, since Rosemary caught pneumonia there.

Rosemary Hoyt (hoyden?) shares her mother's ability to balance "feminine" grief with "masculine" rigidity. In her career, she is able to integrate her "feminine" emotionality with the "hard" nature of her male precursors. Her economic status, Mrs. Speers explains to her, facilitates her ability to remain in emotional control during her relationship with Dick: "You were brought up to work—not especially to marry. . . . Wound yourself or him—whatever happens it can't spoil you because economically you're a boy, not a girl" (TITN, 39). While this advice demonstrates Mrs. Speers's callousness toward Dick, it promotes the only end she is interested in—her daughter's ability to survive hardships. Similarly, Mrs. Speers suggests that Rosemary should watch the duel from a safe distance and "be able to help afterward" (TITN, 47). In other words, like Mrs. Speers's military / medical husbands, Rosemary should leave others to worry about preventing the senseless violence. Instead, she should remain prepared for the lesser emotional burden of limiting the suffering.

Though Rosemary's wage-earning status permits her "masculine" independence, she is able to express her "feminine" concern for others through her work itself. In her film *Daddy's Girl*, as in her personal life, she plays a young woman cut off from her father. The plot is a tearjerker, for it makes "Women . . . forget the dirty dishes at home and weep, even within the picture one woman wept so long that she almost stole the film away from Rosemary" (TITN, 68). As the "feminine" reaction to grief involves an attempt to draw people closer together, the antiseptic ending of the movie involves a "lovely shot of Rosemary and her parent united at last in a father complex so apparent that Dick wince[s] for all psychologists at the vicious sentimentality" (TITN, 69).

Her Electra complex in the movie clearly replicates her personal life, for she clings to Dr. Diver as if he were her father. She feels that he will "take care of her" (TITN, 15), and unlike Nicole, she is consciously drawn to the ("masculine") "layer of hardness in him" (TITN, 18). Desperate for his affections, she expresses her "feminine" grief in his presence, weeping at the slightest provocation. Ultimately, she is able to maintain a reserved affection for him and pursue her "masculine" individualism, for she resumes her movie career and has flings with other men. Thus, in both her career and her personal life, she creatively integrates her opposing traits, successfully living up to her responsibility as a living linking object.

Hysteria and Shell Shock

Through these characters, Fitzgerald explores not only masculine and feminine modes of grief, but also American and English modes. Campion is an Englishman, and all the others are at least in part American. Barban is "less" American than the others though, for Rosemary views him as "unmistakably Latin." Why is there a strong disposition toward melancholy among the Americans and English that differs from Barban's "Latin" cynicism, his successful repression of emotion? Mother-blaming on a vast scale, the narrator alludes to the American part of the problem when he refers to the "illusions of eternal strength and health, and of the essential goodness of people; illusions of a nation, the lies of generations of frontier mothers who had to croon falsely, that there were no wolves outside the cabin door" (TITN, 115–16). The narrator also refers to the "American woman" and her effect on the culture: "[her] clean-sweeping irrational temper that had broken the moral back of a race and made a nursery out of a continent" (TITN, 233). In other words, raised by smothering mothers, Americans fail to develop the capacity for reality testing, for coping with pain. They cling to their illusions of complete security. Another reference is made to the narcissistic self-absorption of Americans in the description of the French train Rosemary travels on: "Unlike American trains that were absorbed in an intense destiny of their own, and scornful of people on another world less swift and breathless, this train was part of the country through which it passed" (TITN, 12). Since such self-absorption inheres with masculinity in the novel, the further implication is that the feminization of American culture leads to its masculinization.[7]

The mention of generations of frontier mothers indicates the cyclical nature of the process. Indeed, Abe's struggle against his "women's world" evokes a common view of an American from a previous generation. Abe shares not only Lincoln's first name, but also his proneness to depression, his premonitory dreams of death, and habit of walking around in a daze. Moreover, Fitzgerald's character and the president share a tendency to withdraw from their more vivacious wives, both named Mary. However, since Lincoln ultimately did not shrink from his wife and his responsibility to others, Abe North hardly achieves the status of Great Emancipator, for he treats the black man Freeman with callousness and remains emotionally distanced from everyone else until his death. While Lincoln ultimately embraced a "feminine" role of promoting harmony and forgiveness of the postbellum South, Abe North does not.[8] In the novel, North represents the norm and Lincoln the exception, for Nicole reflects upon Americans' tendency to "dissipate."

Those Americans who can not avoid the loss of illusions are particularly prone to mental illness. Dick's partner, Franz Gregorovius, proposes that the two of them make their fortune by opening their own clinic for "nervous breakdowns from America" (TITN, 175). The feminization of American culture is so severe, Fitzgerald suggests, that even fathers can demonstrate smothering, "feminine" behavior. In addition to Mr. Warren, Nicole's father-mother, there is the American father of one patient in Dick's clinic who raised his children to believe that "childhood was intended to be all fun" (TITN, 185). The father "tried to protect a nervous brood from life's troubles and had succeeded merely in preventing them from developing powers of adjustment to life's inevitable surprises (TITN, 185–86).

As the Americans took Victorianism to a further extreme than did the English, the English would be less feminine, less prone to emotional unbalance, according to the perspective in the novel. Indeed, Baby Warren states that the English are the "best-balanced race in the world" (TITN, 215). English courteousness lies in between extreme "femininity" and "masculinity." However, in the "broken universe of the war's ending" (TITN, 243), where "masculine" destructiveness has triumphed over the "women's world" of empathy and emotion, anyone unlike Barban, anyone with a "feminine" inclination, would likely struggle with the harshness of life. Accordingly, both Americans and English in the novel are remarkably prone to "nervousness," a condition referred to scores of times. Campion's courteousness seems exaggerated, and he easily loses his emotional balance. When Dick and Rosemary visit an arts exhibition, they encounter a crowd of people, "mostly women," including among them Americans and English whose behavior indicates a "purely nervous inspiration. They were very quiet and lethargic at certain hours and then they exploded into sudden quarrels and breakdowns and seductions" (TITN, 71).

The "masculine" destructiveness ushered in by World War I results also in shell shock / hysteria. In his notes, Fitzgerald entitled book 3 "Casualties." Franz says of his patients, "we have some shell-shocks who merely heard an air raid from a distance. We have a few who merely read newspapers" (TITN, 117). Baby Warren is described as "hysterical with impotence and exhaustion" (TITN, 232) when she lets down her "masculine" facade of emotional coolness and desperately attempts to obtain diplomatic assistance for Dick, as he waits in the Italian jail. Two symptoms of hysteria, fits of sobbing and paralysis, are evoked in the effeminate Campion's copious tears before the duel and his admitted habit of remaining in bed "for days" when trouble arises. Abe North, despondently walking as if "in a slow dream," resembles shell shock victims experiencing recurring nightmares. Overcome with emotion, Abe feels like a "helpless child" instead of a man. Struggling to repress her emotions during an attack of schizophrenia in the hotel bathroom, Nicole experiences a paralytic hysteria, "swaying sidewise and sidewise" in the hotel bathroom at the end of book 1 (TITN, 112). During her first attack in the novel at her home on the Riviera, she was "dissolved in crazy laughter" (TITN, 167), her repressed anxiety returning in a new form. Similarly, in another attack in book 2, Dick finds her "laughing hilariously" (TITN, 189) as she rides on a ferris wheel (more "paralytic" swaying). Bystanders are struck by "the intensity of Nicole's hysteria" (TITN, 189). Having balanced the "feminine" and "masculine" sides of her personality, Rosemary is one American who differs from the others, for she does not experience paralysis after a violent episode in book 1. When an American woman shoots her lover (a sign of the modern "masculinization" of American culture, where even women are destructive), Rosemary in part feels fear, for she wishes that Dick would "make a moral comment on the matter," pacifying her. At the same time, however, she avoids becoming shell shocked; she is "accustomed to having shell-fragments of such events shriek past her head" (TITN, 85), perhaps because she witnessed her medical stepfather attending to patients.

DICK'S RESISTANCE TO SELF-ANALYSIS

The world of "feminine" grief and shell shock seems remote from Dick when he is a young man. He dares to swim the winter Danube, as if he is in disbelief of his mortality. He refers to himself as "Lucky Dick." Fitzgerald's ironic use of this nickname for a tragic character indicates his distance from Dick's self-image (though the distance is not consistently maintained throughout the novel). To be sure, Dick does benefit from good luck at first, for while he is in the military, he is allowed to pursue his studies in Zurich instead of actively taking part in the war. Consequently, he comes to believe that the "war didn't touch him at all" (TITN, 113). His life proceeds swimmingly as he writes a textbook on psychology that is eventually published in six languages. However, despite his seeming invincibility, he says to Franz, "The weakness of this profession is its attraction for the man a little crippled and broken. Within the walls of the profession he compensates by tending toward the clinical, the 'practical'—he has won his battle without a struggle" (TITN, 136–37). His statement, as Berman notes, "hints at a counterphobic motive behind the decision to become a psychiatrist."[9]

Despite Dick's seeming admission, he demonstrates little interest at this point of the novel in plumbing his past for evidence of any counterphobic motive. His lack of introspectiveness does not surprise us, since he later says to Nicole, "Try to forget the past . . ." (TITN, 142)—advice laughable for anyone, especially a psychoanalyst, to provide. His words also resound with dramatic irony when he responds to Baby Warren's inquisitiveness about his family background: "my past is open to investigation" (TITN, 157). The continued dramatic irony indicates Fitzgerald's disapproval of his protagonist's "masculine" repression of the past. A friend once warned Dick about that repressiveness, suggesting that his "memory" was not one of his strong suits, that its weakness would eventually lead him toward "trouble." Though in later years, Dick likes to reflect that his time as a young man served as his "heroic period," the text indicates that this time would be more aptly described as his shallow period.

His lack of introspectiveness fosters his grandiose ambition of becoming a "good psychologist—maybe to be the greatest one that ever lived" (TITN, 130–31). Keeping in mind the psychology of narcissism, we might suspect that his grandiosity exists as a defense against the fear of withheld love. We should consider whether, as the son of a "frontier mother," Dick has struggled with feelings of maternal loss and accordingly clings to his illusions of omnipotence and immortality. Indeed, early in his career, he has a vague sense of his inner anxiety over object love:

> In the dead white hours in Zurich staring into a stranger's pantry across the upshine of a street-lamp, he used to think that he wanted to be good, he wanted to be kind, he wanted to be brave and wise, but it was all pretty difficult. He wanted to be loved, too, if he could fit it in. (TITN, 132)

Consequently, he may be accidentally admitting to something very significant when he attributes his career choice to a trivial circumstance: "I got to be a psychiatrist because there was a girl at St. Hilda's in Oxford that went to the same lectures" (TITN, 137). It may have meant more for him to win her love than he realizes. In book 3 of the novel, when he uncharacteristically adheres to his training in depth psychology and reflects upon his past, he develops insight into his inner concern over object love. He feels that in his relationships with others, their

> personalities had seemed to press up so close to him that he became the personality itself—there seemed some necessity of taking all or nothing; it was as if for the remainder of his life he was condemned to carry with him the egos of certain people, early met and early loved, and to be only as complete as they were complete themselves. There was some element of loneliness involved—so easy to be loved—so hard to love. (TITN, 243)

His consideration of people "early met and early loved" suggests that his thoughts are now directed toward his youth. His need to "carry with him the egos" of others, Berman notes, evokes the preoedipal stage of development in which the "the form of nurturing creates the archetypes of identifications, the basis of future interaction."[10] Berman further glosses, "Dick's insatiable quest for love paradoxically drains him, rendering him broken and incomplete. Emotional involvement proves disastrous because it threatens the distinction between self and other."[11]

DICK'S INFANCY

Berman's allusion to Dick's preoedipal conflict relates to my discussion of mourning. During Dick's infancy and possibly his later childhood, his parents were not "complete"—they had an emptiness in their lives, as we see in another of his belated moments of introspection after he has learned of his father's death:

> Dick loved his father—again and again he referred judgments to what his father would probably have thought or done. Dick was born several months after the death of two young sisters and his father, guessing what would be the effect on Dick's mother, had saved him from a spoiling by becoming his moral guide. He was of tired stock yet he raised himself to that effort. (TITN, 203)

These sentences are culled nearly verbatim from Fitzgerald's memorial essay "The Death of My Father," the only significant difference being the change to third person voice. However, as if to emphasize the importance of familial loss in Dick's past, Fitzgerald makes changes in other parts of the novelized version of the essay. In one change, Fitzgerald veers from autobiography when Dick reflects that his father "died alone," having survived his wife, his brothers, and his sisters. In another change, Fitzgerald takes into account an additional autobiographical fact, alluding to the death of his grandfather in his father's youth. Fitzgerald had written in the essay that his father. Edward, was raised by his "mother and grandmother," while in the novel, he writes that Dick's father was raised by "two proud widows." In the novel, Fitzgerald includes a scene describing Dick's thoughts at the funeral and thus affords us further insight into the importance of familial losses:

> Next day at the churchyard his father was laid among a hundred Divers, Dorseys, and Hunters. It was very friendly leaving him there with all his relations around him. Flowers were scattered on the brown unsettled earth. Dick had no more ties here now and did not believe he would come back. He knelt on the hard soil. These dead, he knew them all, their weather-beaten faces with blue flashing eyes, the sparc violent bodies, the souls made of new earth in the forest-heavy darkness of the seventeenth century.
> 'Good-by, my father—good-by, all my fathers.' (TITN, 205)

Dick surprises us here with his ability to identify with the deceased, to conjure up a vivid image of people who died even before he was born. Somehow, he knows these people, seeing them as if they are alive. He seems prepared to "carry with him the egos" of his forebears.

His previous consideration of the circumstances surrounding his birth illuminates his unusual imaginative ability. If his mother felt a temptation to "spoil" him in the wake of her daughters' deaths, we might say that she saw him as compensation; she transferred her feelings toward them onto him. Transference love, then, existed in Dick's life from the very first. Though Dick feels his father "*saved* him from a spoiling," his mother's role in his upbringing cannot be overlooked.

Moreover, despite what Dick feels, we would expect that his father too would have felt at least some desire to spoil him, to see him as a consolatory linking object. Just pages from the end of the novel, he finally becomes fully conscious of the importance of relatives' deaths in his upbringing. He recalls that it "had early become a habit to be loved, perhaps from the moment when he had realized that he was the last hope of a decaying clan" (TITN, 300). His introspectiveness has never gone so deep as it does now, yet tragically, he has already destroyed his life. As Baby Warren associates her boyfriends with the two men she has lost, as Mrs. Speers associates her daughter with the two men she has survived, so have Dick's parent(s) placed "hope" on him that they had formerly placed on other "clan" members—including especially, we suspect, his two recently deceased sisters.[12]

Dick has had to "carry with him" the "hope" formerly placed on the deceased, the past members of his "decaying" family. Unfortunately, someone who receives such conditional love is encouraged to fear: "I will not receive parental love if I do not fulfill that hope." His sense that it is "so easy to be loved" hints at the problem, for a love intensified by adventitious circumstances can be described as "easy." The fear of withheld parental love helps to explain his anxiety toward others: "[T]heir happiness was his preoccupation, but at the first flicker of doubt as to its all-inclusiveness, he evaporated before their eyes" (TITN, 26). In thus failing to receive an all-inclusive" love, a "fascinated and uncritical" affection (TITN, 26) evocative of parental love, he sinks into an inner "melancholy" (TITN, 26), evocative of parental loss.

This conflict illuminates his decision to become a psychiatrist. He displays his characteristic resistance to self-knowledge when he contrasts himself with Franz, telling him "fate selected you for your profession before you were born" (TITN, 137). Franz is a pathologist, an expert on primal circumstances, and he realizes that he has been drawn toward the field of psychology in order to take after his deceased forebears, pioneers in the field. As a young man, Dick fails to understand the way that circumstances before his birth have similarly contributed to his career aspirations. By becoming a great and famous psychiatrist, he can empathize and merge with his patients, much as the linking object serves as an embodied meeting ground between the mourner and the deceased. Moreover, he can seek to cure his patients, much as the existence of the linking object provides consolation for the mourner. Furthermore, in receiving the profound admiration of his patients, he can cure his sense of parental loss.

If these lofty aspirations encourage a fear of failure, we should consider the possibility that he experiences another fear as well. He might worry that he will become effeminized in assuming the burden of grief. Previous critics have noted Dick's priapism and homophobia, as well as his creator's.[13] Since the desire to empathize and grieve inheres with femininity in his culture, that desire might be difficult for him to accept. In terms of Volkan's theory, we might hypothesize that Dick would struggle to integrate those traits encouraged by his role as living linking object with those masculine traits he considers distinctly his own. Moreover, because Fitzgerald demonstrates an interest, through his depiction of Rosemary, in the way that the living linking object's sense of gender is connected with the gender of the deceased, a portrayal consistent with Volkan's theories, there is also a possibility that Dick's gender identity and fear of that identity are connected to his belief that he must fulfill his parents' hopes in the wake of familial deaths.

Indeed, he does demonstrate a fear of experiencing empathy that contrasts with his inner desire to "carry with him the egos" of others. Rather than admiring Franz's "feminine" desire to care for patients, he admires his partner's repression of emotion, the way his voice comes "not from his nervous system" (TITN, 123) when he speaks to a nurse or patient. Dick demonstrates that he does not want to think of himself as an empathic person. When Rosemary observes that he likes to help people, he claims, "I only pretend to" (TITN, 84). He again downplays his empathic nature in telling Mrs. Speers that his "politeness is only a trick of the heart" (TITN, 163). We see both his caring nature and his resistance to caring when Rosemary finds the body of Peterson in her hotel room. On the one hand, Dick shows a lack of concern over Peterson's death, referring to it as the result of "some nigger scrap" (TITN, 110). In this respect, like Abe North, Dick hardly resembles the Great Emancipator. On the other hand, Dick takes care of Rosemary at this time, seeing to it that her reputation is not sullied by the situation.

We suspect, then, that his disgust at the "vicious sentimentality" of *Daddy's Girl* reflects his disgust with his own caring nature. However, in integrating his father's reserved grief, Dick would be avoiding the extreme "femininity" he fears. For Dick, his father's grief would resemble an amalgam of femininity and masculinity, for he feels his father resisted polarized behavior, including both an innate desire to withdraw from the family and a desire to "spoil" him. Accordingly, in serving as his son's "moral guide," Dick's father passed on values he had learned from women in mourning—the "two proud widows" who had previously raised him. Moreover, Dick's father's values are no doubt related to his profession as a clergyman, a profession that vigorously upheld feminist domestic values in the nineteenth century.[14] Also significantly, Dick's father's values served as a social code of behavior in a "women's world." Soon after arriving in a northern town from his native South during the Era of Reconstruction—a personal and national period of loss—he impressed everyone by entering a crowded room and introducing himself first to a "grey-haired" woman. Thus, his manners led him to recognize the importance of the matriarchal side of society.

To some extent, Dick has appropriated his father's means of coping with loss: "From his father Dick ha[s] learned the somewhat conscious good manners of the young Southerner coming north after the Civil War" (TITN, 163). Consequently, most people who have read Dick's scholarship, Franz states, believe he is "an Englishman—they don't believe that such thoroughness could come out of America" (TITN, 239). They believe he demonstrates too much understanding of the world around him to be a narcissistic American. Franz's wife Kaethe has a similar view, for while she dislikes Americans, she feels Dick is "different, he thinks of others" (TITN, 238). In fact, even though Franz enjoys attending to patients and Dick does not, the latter apparently demonstrates greater clinical empathy, for most of the patients at the clinic prefer to be visited by him. Why they do, we cannot tell, since Fitzgerald successfully demonstrates Dick's empathic nature only in scenes taking place outside the clinic. Still, we can see that there are two opposed sides to Dick's personality: the "unmacho" "English" side, and the "masculine," "American" side.

As he increasingly represses the former side, he eventually demonstrates symptoms of hysteria / shell shock. Repeatedly in the latter half of the novel, we learn of his uncontrolled risibility, his "surging hilarity," his "interior laughter." These emotions are a return of the repressed in a new form. He is able to diagnose his malady, for after dreaming of soldiers' "ghastly," "mutilated" bodies, he wakes up and writes down the diagnosis "Non-combatant's shell-shock" (TITN, 179). His diagnosis is "half-ironic," probably because he believes the war "didn't touch him" and because he has responded with skepticism to Franz's claim that some shell shocks were not in the war. Franz's claim would be valid in "real life," since as Showalter notes, some of the shell shocked had never been exposed to combat. Doctors who at first wished to blame shell shock symptoms on carbon-monoxide poisoning and other organic causes instead of analyzing the soldiers' psyches were confused by these soldiers.[15] Similarly, it is not until late in the novel that Dick succeeds in gaining insight into the lifelong battle within his mind.

DICK'S *TRUE* "HEROIC PERIOD"

However, before his repressive nature and resulting shell shock symptoms become severe, there are brief but important moments where he demonstrates an impressive capacity for empathizing with others and assuming the burden of grief in an uncaring, modern world, thus taking his place among the pantheon of Fitzgeraldian heroes. In its validation of antipatriarchal values, the novel includes an aspect that stands in contrast to its misogynistic aspect. We can see that Fitzgerald intended to include a "feminine" element in *Tender Is the Night*, since in referring to the novel, he wrote to Maxwell Perkins, "I don't think there is a comparison between this book and *The Great Gatsby* as a seller. *The Great Gatsby* had against it its length and its purely masculine interest. This book, on the contrary, is a woman's book."[16] While his statement about *The Great Gatsby* is misleading—Nick and Gatsby's devotion to mourning outweighs the implicit criticism of Daisy's grief and implicit satire of Myrtle's "seance"—*Tender Is the Night* does provide a more direct and detailed endorsement of "feminine" values.

In book 1, Dick provides his friends and acquaintances, all of them touched by loss, with relief from their unhappiness. He produces a miracle cure for them when they congregate at his home overlooking the "decaying Riviera," a fitting home for a man who was raised in a "decaying clan." Born to parents distracted by prior deaths, he hosts a party where "person by person . . . give[s] up something, a preoccupation, an anxiety, a suspicion, and now they [are] only their best selves" (TITN, 31). As Mrs. Speers was drawn toward Rosemary in reaction to loss, Rosemary finds that she has a "conviction of homecoming" (TITN, 33) in witnessing the emotionally troubled people at the party sympathizing with each other to a greater degree than they have before in the novel. As Mrs. Speers has found consolation in seeing to it that her daughter takes on her husbands' traits, Rosemary now assumes the reserved parental behavior of her father and stepfather—she feels "eager for the others' enjoyment, as if they were her future stepchildren" (TITN, 32). In the "diffused magic" of the air and above the "ghostly" Mediterranean below, Rosemary experiences a supernatural vision while sitting at Dick's table with the others, much like a participant at a seance contacting a deceased loved one: "The table seemed to have risen a little toward the sky like a mechanical dancing platform, giving the people around it a sense of being alone with each other in the dark universe" (TITN, 33). Dick, it seems, is able to turn tables and to effect levitation, thus taking on the role, traditionally performed by women, of medium presiding over a "seance." He steers everyone present toward the tender night beyond death. However, he is lucky to pull off his magic trick, for as they are "lifted" into the "rarer atmosphere of sentiment" (TITN, 33), the party breaks up, and McKisco and Barban soon after get into their disagreement on the way home and arrange for their duel. Dick has in part wished for this destruction of "sentiment," since he has previously stated, "I want to give a really *bad* party" (TITN, 26).

His "masculine" side has opposed the emotional closeness displayed during the party, though for a brief time, his heroic side prevailed.

"Masculinity" has destroyed more than just his party, as we see when Dick visits the site of the Battle of Somme with Abe and Rosemary. Despite or because Abe was in the war, he displays scant concern over the battle that involved an unparalleled degree of destructiveness, even by World War I standards. In contrast, Dick states that the battle represented more than just the senseless slaughter, the "mass butchery," that "General Grant invented":

> "This western-front business couldn't be done again, not for a long time. The young men think they could do it but they couldn't. They could fight the first Marne again but not this. This took religion and years of plenty and tremendous sureties and the exact relation that existed between the classes. The Russians and Italians weren't any good on this front. You had to have a whole-souled sentimental equipment going back further than you remember. You had to remember Christmas, and postcards of the Crown Prince and his fiancee, and little cafes in Valence and beer gardens in Unter den Linden and weddings at the mairie, and going to the derby, and your grandfather's whiskers." (TITN, 56)

Once again, he conjures up images of the deceased, demonstrating his sense of kinship with the past. He has a sense that the soldiers who entered the battle did not simply intend to "tear things apart," as men in his society do. Rather, they fought because they cared about others, because they wished to preserve their familial and social traditions. Punctuating his thoughts, he adds, "This was the last love battle" (TITN, 56). His vision of these men thus parallels his belief in his father's resistance to ("masculine") individualism. Recognizing on some level the connection between the battle and his own background and identity, he "mourn[s] persistently," "All *my* beautiful lovely safe world blew itself up here with a great gust of high explosive love" (TITN, 57; emphasis mine).

Though he sees the battle as a metaphor for the destruction of his world, he still maintains his code of values when he notices a woman at the site expressing grief. She is troubled because she cannot place her wreath on her brother's grave, unable to find it among the masses of graves. He approaches and advises her to place the wreath on any grave, further demonstrating his desire to recognize the soldiers' ("feminine") camaraderie instead of dwelling only on the battle's destructiveness. He then takes it upon himself to lift the woman's spirits on the way back to Paris. Given his experience with sibling loss, it is understandable that he would be able to empathize with hers. Though Abe has gently mocked Dick's view of the conflict—likening his love battle metaphor to something from D. H. Lawrence—Dick comes across as the more impressive character in this passage. He understands the barbarism ultimately involved in this battle and can therefore appreciate Abe's modernistic sense of emptiness, yet he refuses to become emotionally numbed—shell shocked, as it were.

Soon after this excursion, he momentarily wavers in his attitude. As he walks through Paris, the interior monologue reveals his reflection upon his role in life:

Rosemary saw him always as a model of correctness. . . . But Dick's necessity of behaving as he did was a projection of some submerged reality: he was compelled to walk there, or stand there, his shirt-sleeve fitting his wrist and his coat sleeve encasing his shirt-sleeve like a sleeve valve, his collar molded plastically to his neck, his red hair cut exactly, his hand holding his small brief case like a dandy—just as another man once found it necessary to stand in front of a church in [Canossa], in sackcloth and ashes. Dick was paying some tribute to things unforgotten, unshriven, unexpurgated. (TITN, 91)

In thinking of Henry IV doing penitence for Pope Gregory, Dick is unconsciously thinking of his need to follow his father's genteel, religious code of "correctness," and this code provides him with a sense of being a "dandy." Later that same day, however, he does not demonstrate his anxiety over becoming effeminized when he sees a group of Americans composed of a polite, "secretarial" man and a number of women. Though he at first feels disgust at this microcosm of the American "women's world," he suddenly feels strongly drawn to that world when he realizes the women are in mourning. They have come to France to commemorate their husbands and sons who died in the war. Dick reflects that in their happy faces, the dignity that surrounded and pervaded the party, he perceived all the maturity of an older America. For a while the sobered women who had come to mourn for their dead, for something they could not repair, made the room beautiful. Momentarily, he sat again on his father's knee, riding with [General Mosby] while the old loyalties and devotions fought on around him. Almost with an effort he turned back to his two women at the table and faced the whole new world in which he believed." (TITN, 100)

He is drawn toward their sense of loss, which stands in contrast to the self-absorption of a "newer America." Their "feminine" grief brings them closer together, for they all look alike: "neither young nor old nor of any particular class" (TITN, 100). Since his father's devotion to the past evokes "feminine" grief, it is not surprising that the sight of these women leads him to remember his father's Civil War storytelling.

Thus far, Dick has not reflected directly upon the origins of his attraction to the bereaved members of an "older America." He resembles the soldiers he sees in book 2, who represent a "lost magnificence, a past effort, a *forgotten* sorrow" (TITN, 200; emphasis mine). Though the soldiers remind him of two of his own losses, his "youth of ten years ago" (TITN, 200) and Abe's death, it is not until that night, when he learns of his father's death from his hotel in Innsbruck, that he consciously dwells upon the largely "forgotten" familial losses dating back further. After checking into his hotel, he passes a statue of the Emperor Maximilian "knelt in prayer above his bronze mourners" (TITN, 200), but the sight fades quickly under the setting sun—a fading symbolic of Dick's hazy perception of his own penitential, grieving attitude toward the world left behind. After his father's funeral, he will wear a black arm band, an anachronistic ritual hinting again at his desire to adhere to the mores of the past.

TURNING INWARD

By this time, however, he has already begun to destroy himself. With his increasing disposition toward faulty empathy and resistance to introspection, his desire to care can emerge only in brief bursts of emotion, bursts so powerful that they imperil his marriage and career. He desires so strongly to console the grieving woman at the sight of the Battle of the Somme that he eventually begins to flirt with her. Similarly, he kisses a female patient in "an idle, almost indulgent way" (TITN, 187). Moreover, when he visits another patient, Fitzgerald writes, "in the awful majesty of her pain he went out to her unreservedly, almost sexually" (TITN, 185). His feelings of disgust in viewing *Daddy's Girl* most likely result not only from fear of his emotional nature, but also from fear of his related desire to substitute for the daddies Rosemary has lost.

His relationship with his patient Nicole has of course marked his first departure from the ethics of his profession and the reparative values learned from his father. After he attempts to sever emotional ties with her in the beginning of their relationship, it is ironically appropriate that he becomes further entangled with her after "accidentally" encountering her on a cable car with Mount Chillon in view above him. In writing that Dick "turns inward" upon spotting Mount Chillon, Fitzgerald again is thinking of his own father. He alludes to "The Prisoner of Chillon," the poem Edward Fitzgerald read to him as a child in which the speaker is locked in a dungeon atop Chillon with his father and brothers, all of them persecuted for their religious convictions. While the speaker in Byron's poem—after his father and brothers die in the dungeon—avoids his sense of loss and confinement by turning inward, exploring the mystical wilderness of his mind and thus heroically continuing his family's spiritual tradition, Dick now unheroically becomes caught up in his countertransferential desire, a perversion of both his professional empathy and his father's religious code, by becoming romantically involved with his grieving patient.[17] He admits to Franz that his attraction to Nicole is intensified by his awareness of her mental anguish: "I'm not as hard-boiled as you are yet; when I see a beautiful shell like [Nicole] I can't help feeling regret about what's inside it" (TITN, 118).

In the Chillon scene, Nicole moves to Dick's section of the cable car after learning that her section was also the "hearse part." Her desire to avoid the hearse section symbolizes her wish to escape from her sense of parental loss. Her unresolved grief lends itself to his countertransference. While there existed an inversion of the parent-child relationship in Dick's infancy, such that he served as "parent," as family rescuer, his relationship with the childlike Nicole similarly undergoes an inversion. She becomes the more aggressive one when they first become involved with each other. Though she has initially seen him as a surrogate mother, he transforms her into a parent, providing her with children, leading her to accept responsibility for them, and meanwhile, becoming a "child" himself through his increasing immaturity. As if sharing his protagonist's countertransference toward Nicole, Fitzgerald concerns himself throughout the novel with her potential as a parent. Though as Berman has noted, Nicole "rarely seems mentally ill to us and never psychotic except for perhaps in a few moments," she does seem "schizophrenic" metaphorically, in that one part of her desires to act like a parent and another part fears the anxiety involved in that role.[18]

Significantly, Fitzgerald includes the following exchanges between Dick and Nicole in their very first conversation within the novel:

> "At present I don't seem to be interested in anything except my work," [Dick says].
> "Oh, I think that's fine for a man," she said quickly. "But for a girl I think she ought to have lots of minor accomplishments and pass them on to her children."
> "I suppose so," said Dick with deliberated indifference. (TITN, 141)

He fails to maintain his appearance of indifference, for moments later, he tells her, "You can have a perfectly normal life with a houseful of beautiful descendants" (TITN, 142). Fittingly, as he thinks of her emotional pain at the end of the scene, his view of her is an oral one, an image characteristic of the novel and Fitzgerald's fiction in general. He finds himself "feeling her unhappiness, and wanting to drink the rain that touched her cheek" (TITN, 143).[19]

After they marry, she continues to struggle with parental anxiety, as we see in several moments of her brief stream-of-consciousness recollection of her relationship with Dick. When she thinks of her first convalescence, she frets over the fact that another woman in the hospital gave birth to a blue baby. She feels the baby would be "much better dead" (TITN, 158). She remains preoccupied with loss, for when she and Dick travel to western Italy, she senses the "dead watching from up on those hills" (TITN, 159). Then, in a rare moment where we possibly glimpse her psychosis, she remembers that "everything got dark again" (TITN, 160) upon her second child's birth. In perhaps a schizophrenic reaction, she thinks, "You tell me my baby is black—that's farcical, that's very cheap" (TITN, 160). We later learn that she went through a "long relapse" after the second child's birth.

Repeatedly, she resembles a grieving / anxious parent. In a passage of interior monologue, Rosemary makes a connection between her grieving mother's withdrawn nature and Nicole's behavior: "It was quiet alone with Nicole—Rosemary found it even quieter than with her mother" (TITN, 17). Appropriately, Mrs. Speers is the one to marvel over Nicole's garden, for Nicole's pampering of her garden parallels Mrs. Speers's grief-related fears for Rosemary's health. Dick says of the garden, "She won't let it alone—she nags it all the time, worries about its diseases. Any day now I expect to have her come down with Powdery Mildew or Fly Speck, or Late Blight" (TITN, 27). Dick thus believes that Nicole's anxiety over the garden will weaken her, much as Mrs. Speers struggles, and Dick's father struggled, to continue on with life in the wake of multiple family losses.

Through Abe, we gain another glimpse of Nicole as parent. When he looks to the top of a staircase and sees her with her children, he stands and watches instead of greeting her, as if transfixed by this lofty tableau. He feels she is "self-revelatory" as she struggles to find the stamina to attend to her parental responsibility, as she stands there "frowning, thinking of her children, less gloating over them than merely animally counting them—a cat checking her cubs with a paw" (TITN, 80). He has called upon her so that she can act like a parent to him, can help him fight through his sense of loss and board the ship to America. He is attempting to "play the helpless child in front of a woman" (TITN, 81).

Since she is a "permanent eccentric," she will never com-

pletely accept her role in the novel as a mother. She is "bringing up children she [can] only pretend gently to love, guided
orphans" (TITN, 180). Thus, like Dick's mother, she is portrayed as someone whose anxiety causes her parental love to
become "easy," insincere, capable of being retracted at any
time. Significantly, when she becomes hysterical and runs
away at the carnival, she runs not only from Dick but also from
her children, who have been there beside them. When Dick
tracks her down and tells her that they must go home, her response is eerie: "Home! . . . And sit and think we're all rotting
and the children's ashes are rotting in every box I open? That
filth!" (TITN, 190). She thinks of her children as if they are
dead. She now seems to have touched upon the heart of her
problem, for her exclamation proves momentarily cathartic.
She feels "sterilized" and begs Dick to help her. However, as
he attempts to figure out where the children are, Nicole struggles again with her emotions, standing apart from him, "evil-
eyed . . . denying the children" (TITN, 191). Later when they
are driving home, she experiences another paroxysm of emotion. She seizes control of the steering wheel and veers the car
off a cliff into a tree, all the while "laughing hilariously" (hys-
terically). Dick loses his temper only when he sees the
"strained faces of the children, looking from parent to parent"
(TITN, 192). Suddenly he feels an urge to "grind her grinning
mask into jelly" (TITN, 192). As he and Nicole stand beside
some men who have come to recover the car, and as the children stand at the top of the cliff, he commands, "Go and wait
with the children, Nicole" (TITN, 193).

Though he feels she will never recover completely from her
mental illness, she does learn in the final book of the novel to
fulfill her parental obligation without experiencing anxiety.
When she and her family visit Mary North's new husband and
stepchildren, she unites with her husband in an argument con-
cerning her elder child. Lanier, the elder child, has told his
father that he was bathed in the same dirty bathwater as
Mary's stepson, and Nicole responds before Dick does. She is
"immediately on guard" (TITN, 258), frightened that her son
will catch the stepson's illness. When Mary later disputes
Dick's accusation that the bathwater was dirty, Nicole rushes
to her husband's defense, attempting to "hold things together"

as she believes a woman should. Afterward, Dick reflects that his family is "unified again" and worries about whether the togetherness will last.

Though the family does not remain together for long, Nicole continues to fulfill her sense of parental responsibility without anxiety. After Dick embarrasses himself on T. F. Golding's yacht, she feels an urge to take care of him. "It would give me so much pleasure"—she says—"to think of a little something I could do for you, Dick" (TITN, 271). By initiating an argument, however, he childishly resists her attempt to help him. Now that she has become a parent to Dick, he experiences jealousy when she nurtures Tommy. Over Dick's objection, she allows Tommy to take home the entire jar of camphor rub for his sore throat. Dick responds to this seemingly trivial incident by childishly staring at the ceiling and then expressing his resentment toward her after she shows pity for him. Nicole feels that he has now become desperate, and indeed, we later learn that Dick feels the marriage is finished after this incident: "from the episode of the camphor-rub, Dick had anticipated everything" (TITN, 308).

Though he feels personally victimized by her attention to Tommy, he also feels that his "case" is "finished." We can see why he feels this way, for in accordance with his unconscious wish, she has learned to cope with the experience of losing an increasingly childish husband, and she now turns without fear to another "child." Tommy's boyish name and sudden lack of individualistic machismo when conversing with her hint at his inner desire to receive care. Though he tells Dick that he intends to serve as her "protector," we expect that will not be the case, for she is financially independent, and she now views *him* as subservient. She "greet[s] Tommy as if he were one of many men at her feet, walking ahead of him instead of beside him" (TITN, 289). She is not troubled by the fact that she will only "be able to hold him so long" (TITN, 294), that he will not need her support forever. She can now accept the experience of losing an "infant" without relapsing into illness. She feels "cured" because her ambivalent, "schizophrenic," parental anxiety no longer controls her behavior.

Thus, her grieving nature is balanced with a "masculine" sense of independence. Interestingly, she has always shown "masculine" potential. As an infant, she displayed little separation anxiety, for Mr. Warren has explained, "I used to hear my wife say she was the only one of our children who never cried at night" (TITN, 125). Moreover, when "traveling with her failing mother" later in her childhood, Nicole devised a clever system of numbering and cataloging everything they carried with them, a system resembling that of a "regimental supply officer" (TITN, 256). Thus, as an officer must balance his "masculine" concern over war with a "feminine" concern for his charges' needs, Nicole learned to serve as "mother and father both" to her mother. Now as an adult, she regains her balanced nature.

RESCUING AND WANDERING

In contrast, Dick can not maintain his emotional balance. As he develops symptoms of hysteria / shell shock, repressing his "unmanly" compulsion to grieve, he makes only scattered attempts to play his lifelong role of familial rescuer. Fitzgerald writes that after Dick's encounter with a "lost and miserable family of two girls and their mother" (TITN, 206),

> An overwhelming desire to help, or to be admired, came over him: he showed them fragments of gaiety; tentatively he bought them wine, with pleasure saw them begin to regain their proper egotism. He pretended they were this and that, and falling in with his own plot, and drinking too much to sustain the illusion, and all this time the women thought only that this was a windfall from heaven. (TITN, 206–7)

The survivor of two sisters and the son of a grieving mother, Dick becomes a "windfall from heaven" for these three women, magically transforming himself into the father of the family and temporarily curing their sense of bereavement.

After he is imprisoned briefly for fighting with the member of the carabinieri, he lies about the cause of his injuries to Nicole and, in so doing, again reveals his fantasies. He claims he attempted to come to the "rescue of a drunken friend" (TITN, 240). Later, his arrival at T. F. Golding's party derives from a sudden urge to see if the people there are "happy." However,

in embarrassing himself by drunkenly insulting guests, his resistance to empathy influences the outcome of his mission. In a
subsequent scene, however, he pulls off one final rescue, helping Mary North and Lady Sibly-Biers to gain freedom after
they are imprisoned for making homosexual advances toward
two other women. In so doing he conquers his resistance,
fighting off a "tendency to ironic laughter" (more of his hysterical symptoms) over the affair. Appropriately, it is when he
goes to free them that he makes a connection between his need
to help others and his role as the last hope of a decaying clan.

While he generally represses his "unmanly" role at the end
of the novel, his attitude toward his children becomes overly
"feminine." He has held a theory that the parent must take
special care not to spoil the child. He feels that "the forcing of
children and the fear of forcing them were inadequate substi-
tutes for the long, careful watchfulness" (TITN, 254). Thus, he
demonstrates once again his allegiance to his father, who, he
believes, avoided Mrs. Diver's spoiling behavior and also
avoided a desire to withdraw from family life. Dick has raised
his children "not to cry or laugh with abandon . . ." (TITN,
255). Their odd lack of strong emotions thus contrasts with
Dick's long-held desire to empathize with others' grief. However, probably because he increasingly represses his emotions
in other aspects of his life, he eventually clings to his children.
They become the center of his life, providing him with his only
sense of "purposefulness." Eventually, he turns to his children
"not protectively but for protection" (TITN, 278). In other
words, he once again inverts a parent-child relationship, encouraging them to take care of him. Nicole, a victim of a parent
so smothering that he became incestuous, is able to perceive
Dick's "almost unnatural interest in the children" (TITN, 265).
His parental attitude now smacks of the smothering, incestuous countertransference he previously displayed toward Nicole.

Significantly, while he is not troubled by his "unnatural" attitude toward his daughter—he is "glad" to have "given so
much" to her—he is "more uncertain" about his behavior
toward his son. We can understand why he is concerned more
about his son, for he considers it especially important for males
to be able to hold back their emotions. Unfortunately, his own

attempts to do so have led to a sort of hysteria, a difficulty in communicating with others, including lovers, friends, and patients—hence his decision to depart for America and cease practicing psychiatry. Thus, he has failed to assimilate the "masculine" identity that he views as distinctly his own with the grieving, empathic identity his parents initially envisioned for him as a living linking object. In refusing to combat his hysteria / shell shock at the end of the novel, he is punishing himself for eventually failing to embrace his parents' hopes for him. Accordingly, his moments of self-destructiveness, including his exile from others at the end of the novel, involve a refusal to gratify his infantile oral hunger, his need to be cared for: "All people want"—Mary North says to him—"is to have a good time and if you make them unhappy you cut yourself off from nourishment" (TITN, 311).[20]

The final paragraphs of the novel indicate the effects of that refusal on his life. Ultimately, he does not "ask for the children to be sent to America" (TITN, 313). Only his incestuous flirtatiousness with younger women continues in America, for he is still "admired by the ladies" and becomes "entangled" with a "girl" at one point. Ultimately, as Nicole loses track of his whereabouts, it becomes clear that he will likely wander around upstate New York, moving from one place to another for the rest of his life. Such wandering around the region in which he was raised suggests he is acting out on his desire to be loved.[21] Fitzgerald's understated satire at the end of the novel indicates his renewed detachment from his protagonist's hysterical repression of grief.[22] While no other work by Fitzgerald demonstrates such a deep fear of mourning's "unmanliness," this remarkably introspective novel provides a heartfelt endorsement of the importance of mourning.

7

The Last Tycoon:
Art as Collaborative Healing

> Story—A hole or bag in which someone finds all the things
> he's ever lost.
>
> —*The Notebooks of F. Scott Fitzgerald*

Fɪᴛᴢɢᴇʀᴀʟᴅ's ᴜɴғɪɴɪꜱʜᴇᴅ ɴᴏᴠᴇʟ, ᴡʜɪᴄʜ ɪꜱ ᴜꜱᴜᴀʟʟʏ ʀᴇꜰᴇʀʀᴇᴅ
to as *The Last Tycoon,* illustrates the importance of creativity
and interdependence in working through mourning. Appropriately, Fitzgerald's relationships with others aided his writing
of the novel during a time of loss in his life. He turned to Sheilah Graham and Budd Schulberg in order to gain insider information about Hollywood. Most likely, Graham, who according
to Fitzgerald's friends, bore a striking resemblance to Zelda,
and Schulberg, a recent college graduate, further "collabo-
rated" with him by helping him to work through his grief for
his wife and daughter back East, Zelda struggling with her in-
curable schizophrenia and Scottie at Vassar. Graham also
helped him to quit drinking, a habit undoubtedly encouraged
by his losses. In receiving others' concern, then, Fitzgerald was
in better condition to write. He poured much of his remaining
energy into the novel. Appropriately, in the novel, a young
woman named Cecilia Brady, a character whom Fitzgerald
noted was based on both his daughter and Schulberg, attempts
to provide emotional support for Monroe Stahr, a prominent
movie producer intensely committed to his work, who mourns
for his deceased wife, Minna, an actress. Also appropriately,
Stahr finds added interest in life through his relationship with
Kathleen Moore, the character based on Graham, whom Stahr
feels at first to be Minna returned from the dead. As part of the

process of working through his grief, he comes to appreciate the fact that Kathleen is not Minna, that Minna will never return.

Thus, after creating ambivalent depictions earlier in his career of characters who compare someone with the object of their grief, Fitzgerald was now favorably depicting a situation in which a character based largely on himself (and also on the late producer Irving Thalberg) was acting similarly. Whereas in "Crazy Sunday," Joel views Stella as someone calculatingly turning him into her deceased husband's double, *The Last Tycoon* suggests that circumstances can make it difficult to avoid such behavior. Stahr cannot blame himself for seeing a close physical resemblance between Minna and Kathleen. Perhaps, then, Fitzgerald was better able at this point in his life to appreciate the fact that his parents, in viewing him as a replacement for their daughters, were also faced with difficult choices in a difficult situation. Accordingly, in conceiving characters for the novel, he appears to have been envisioning the "good-enough" grieving parent rather than the "all-good" or "all-bad" one, as if he found it less difficult now to accept his parents as complex people attempting to cope with loss in the best way they could. His mother had died in 1936, five years after his father's death, and three years before he began this novel—circumstances that would likely have intensified his desire to seek reparation with them.[1] In his notes, Fitzgerald writes of the personal history of Thalia, the original name for Kathleen's character:

> One of the children of the first marriage died. It was blamed on her because if the divorce had not occurred and she hadn't appeared, it would not have happened. Her husband went all to pieces, lost all his money and she is still taking care of him in a vague way and he is perhaps in a sanitarium in the East and perhaps dead.[2]

Whether or not Fitzgerald continued to feel he should include these circumstances in the novel (no reference to them occurs in the published text), it is significant that he considered them in the first place. While these circumstances recall Fitzgerald's separation from his daughter and Zelda's institutionalization, and also recall Sheilah Graham's attempt to rise up from humble origins, they recall no circumstances more strongly than those of his parents in his childhood: Edward's chronic grief over the loss of his daughters, then more grief over financial losses, and finally, Mollie's renewal of vitality, her attempt to master her emotions and take control of the future author's upbringing. Appropriately, when Stahr first catches a glimpse of Kathleen, the scene takes places on the movie lot where assorted props and sets are scattered about, a disarray reminiscent of "the torn picture books of childhood." And at the time, Hollywood has just been hit by an earthquake, which Cecilia describes as "some nightmare attempt to attach our navel cords again and jerk us back to the womb of creation" (LT, 23). Because Kathleen enters his life at this time, the regressive "nightmare" turns to a dream. And eventually, Kathleen becomes "good-enough" rather than the embodiment of his dream. Stahr learns to cease idealizing her as a double for Minna, and he also accepts the fact that she is preoccupied with another matter.[3] He acknowledges in turn that his lost love object has been idealized, made larger-than-life, for he tells Kathleen: "You look more like she actually *looked* than how she was on the screen" (LT, 90).

We are also reminded of the "good-enough" parent in another character in the text. While working on the novel, Fitzgerald wrote a sketch entitled "Dearly Beloved," where he sympathetically portrays a character who recalls Edward Fitzgerald. And that character, as Bruccoli notes, "has obvious connections with the philosophical black fisherman in *The Last Tycoon*."[4] In the sketch, a young black man, committed to self-improvement, marries an equally ambitious woman. Around the time that their son is born, the father slips under a train and loses his leg—an unmanning event. The parents become consumed with grief, wishing the leg would somehow grow back, that their dream of success would be untouched by the cruelties of life. They are able to provide their son with only "spare-time love," and an aunt takes care of him. Thus, Fitzgerald writes here of a situation that strongly evokes his parents' preoccupation with grief, including his father's "unmanly" loss of vitality. We are also reminded of his aunt's role in providing him with "discipline." Interestingly, the narration in the sketch is extremely sentimental. In the first sentence, the protagonist is directly addressed: "O my Beauty Boy—reading Plato so divine!"[5] Fitzgerald's tone is not surprising, given the highly personal subject matter.

The fisherman in the novel is also a parent, and though not noticeably in mourning, he becomes an authoritative figure in Stahr's life, in keeping with the pervasive tradition in American literature in which a black male character serves as a parental figure for a white male.[6] The fisherman suggests that the movies have little intellectual value for himself and his children, and Stahr takes into account his view. Stahr deepens his commitment to making important movies, as if internalizing the parent into his superego, much as Dick, the son of a clergyman, has done in *Tender Is the Night*.

MOVIEMAKING AND EMPATHY

In a sense, then, it appears that Fitzgerald's parents were involved in the collaborative effort behind the writing of *The Last Tycoon*. Appropriately, his protagonist promotes the cause of "collaboration"—of empathy and communal healing. As the inventor of a system where multiple writers work on a script concurrently, an extension of the collaborative effort of moviemaking as a whole, Stahr finds himself at odds with writers who wish to work alone, transforming their personal visions into esoteric works of art. Fitzgerald writes that when Stahr and his employees view the day's filming in order to decide what to edit, "Dreams hung in fragments at the far end of the room, suffered analysis, passed—to be dreamed in crowds, or else discarded" (LT, 56).

The writer George Boxley receives a pat on the shoulder from Stahr when he finally begins to understand Stahr's cinematic sensibility. In a meeting, Boxley explains his sudden idea about a movie in development: "We don't need *less* characters . . . We need *more*" (LT, 108). He outlines a theme they should pursue in the movie: "Let each character see himself in the other's place . . . The policeman is about to arrest the thief when he sees that the thief actually has *his* face. . . . You could almost call the thing 'Put Yourself in My Place' " (LT, 108). Boxley envisions a movie in which the characters empathize with each other, a reflection of his own collaboration with the other writers in this scene.

Like the characters in Boxley's envisioned movie, Stahr puts himself in the place of others. As the last tycoon, he "steps outside" his working class, Jewish origins (both elements of his background were shared by Thalberg and Graham). He preserves a part of history not his own in advocating the importance of a "monarch" in charge of movie production instead of a system where the unions have greater power; he has "just managed to climb out of a thousand years of Jewry into the late eighteenth century. He [can] not bear to see it melt away—he cherishe[s] the parvenu's passionate loyalty to an imaginary past" (LT, 119). Moreover, though Stahr envisions himself as an aristocrat from the past, he steps out of that role and also puts himself in the place of his employees, empathizing with their problems: "[H]ere was Stahr to care, for all of them" (LT, 43). Given his empathic role, it is appropriate that Fitzgerald placed the novel several years in the past, during the Depression. Thus, the novel also takes place at a time when the Nazis were intensifying their persecution of Jews. Both the distressing events in America and Germany are alluded to in the novel. The major conflict in the novel was to involve Stahr's struggle against another Hollywood mogul, Cecilia's father, who cares only about himself. As Fitzgerald explains in a synopsis of his planned novel, Brady is "the monopolist at its worst," someone "not interested in the making of pictures save as it will benefit his bank account" (LT, xxxii, xxxiii). Stahr, in contrast, is willing to put financial considerations on the backburner if he sees that an important movie can be produced.[7] The ending of the novel was to involve Stahr's tragic death in a plane crash caused by a bomb in the cargo hold, the result of Brady's contract on his rival's life.

STAHR AND OTHER FITZGERALDIAN HEROES

We might see Stahr as "more heroic" than his predecessors in previous Fitzgerald texts. Gatsby's grief for Daisy, though impressive in its intensity, evoked an infantile desire for magical omnipotence. In order for Gatsby to feel satisfied, it was necessary for Daisy to deny her past preoccupation with others, to state that she never loved Tom and loved only Gatsby, effectively erasing years of history, including the crucial event of Pammy's birth. In contrast, Stahr's acceptance of Kathleen's past and his identification with a political history formerly sealed off to him demonstrate his maturity. Moreover, while Amory Blaine, Anthony Patch, Nick Carraway, and Dick Diver fear becoming effeminized in experiencing grief and empathy, Stahr betrays no such fear. Furthermore, whereas other Fitzgerald characters confront the depths of their grief, Stahr is determined not only to confront it but also to work through it. He recognizes that he cannot cling forever to the past as a substitute for the present, that his memories are already loosening their hold on him. As he sees a young couple disappear into the summer twilight, he thinks, "Little by little he was losing the feel of such things, until it seemed that Minna had taken their poignancy with her; his apprehension of splendor was fading so that presently the luxury of eternal mourning would depart" (LT, 62). Though he had been in "love with Minna and death together" (LT, 97), he now finds value in the world around him in falling in love with Kathleen. And though he does not express his commitment to Kathleen, he resists doing so not because he is ambivalent toward moving on with his life, but because producing movies is his greatest love, his consuming interest. He pours tremendous energy into his work, explaining to Kathleen, "Pictures are my girl" (LT, 71). And eventually, he was to continue working and to renew his relationship with Kathleen before his death.

STAHR'S PROJECTION ROOM

At the beginning of the novel, a character named Manny Schwartze responds self-destructively to his sense of loss. He commits suicide at the historical landmark of Andrew Jackson's home, an action that Cecilia interprets as an effort to reunite with his originary love object: "It was doubtful if he knew who Andrew Jackson was as he wandered around, but perhaps he figured that . . . [Jackson] was large and merciful, able to understand. At both ends of life man needed nourishment—a breast—a shrine" (LT, 13). In contrast, because of the creative nature of his work, we might see Stahr's passion for moviemaking as his attempt to respond creatively to loss, to reunite temporarily with Minna through the world of art. Rather than concluding that the novel is about "the struggle to abandon illusions and enter into life,"[8] we might see it as about the power of illusions to lessen the trauma of loss and facilitate the process of working through. Stahr's devotion to the movies resembles the infant's use of "transitional objects" and "transitional phenomena" as a way of coping with maternal separation. Psychoanalyst D. W. Winnicott, who coined these terms, has found that every infant is "capable of conceiving of the idea of something that would meet the growing need that arises out of instinctual tension," a tension especially noticeable during the weaning process.[9] A blanket or a teddy bear often serves as the item to relieve the tension. Such an item is a transitional object. A transitional phenomenon, such as an infant's babbling or singing, also helps to relieve separation anxiety. No individual ever completely progresses beyond the need for transitional phenomena. Those adults who absorb themselves in the arts, Winnicott suggests, are creating a transitional space between illusion and disillusion, denial and acceptance of anxiety.

While the transitional object is similar to the Volkanian linking object in that both serve as responses to separation, they differ in several ways, one of which is relevant to the present concern. As Volkan notes, infants cling to their transitional objects "all the time," while pathological mourners generally keep their linking objects out of sight, remaining distanced from their grief.[10] Like the former, but unlike the later, Fitzgerald's protagonist devotes himself to moviemaking, working night and day. And when Stahr sits in his projection room at one point, viewing the day's filming of various movies in development, he further resembles infants clinging to their transitional objects, for he exists in a neutral space between psychic and external reality; life with Minna and life without. He sees on the screen a prop representing Siva, the god of death and life, as if in producing a mainstream movie for others to appreciate, he has projected his private fantasy of Minna's reincarnation onto the screen. Previously, the prop, a symbol of art, figured as part of another transitional phenomenon. When Stahr first glimpsed Minna's "ghost" (Kathleen) at the beginning of the novel, she was crouching atop that movie prop in order to avoid getting soaked in a flood resulting from the earthquake. Stahr stood and stared transfixed.

FITZGERALD'S "SUPERNATURAL" ART

Like Stahr's vision of Minna on the head of Siva, Fitzgerald's fiction served a supernaturalistic function. Through his writings, he had the ability to bring characters into existence—good, bad, and "good-enough" parents, as well as good, bad, and "good-enough" sons. And though, or because, he never knew his elder sisters, he even brought them into existence, it seems, through his depiction of Eleanor in *This Side of Paradise* and Margery Lee in "The Ice Palace." The worlds he depicted in his fiction, where verisimilitude and fantasy converged, served as alternatives to his often turbulent life. He once wrote in one of his notebooks, "I can never remember the times when I wrote anything—This Side of Paradise time or Beautiful and Damned and Gatsby for instance. Lived in a story."[11]

Much as Stahr sees his aesthetic vision as universal, Fitzgerald realized that his autobiographically based fiction spoke to others. Fitzgerald once wrote, speaking of himself in the third person, that the Jazz Age "bore him up, flattered him and gave him more money than he had dreamed of, simply for telling people that he felt as they did."[12] Though readers in subsequent years failed to support him so fervently, recent generations have similarly identified with his writings and have provided him with the admiration he had craved since his infancy.

Notes

INTRODUCTION

1. See Norman N. Holland, *The I* (New Haven: Yale University Press, 1985): 23–33; Richard A. Koenigsberg, "F. Scott Fitzgerald: Literature and the Work of Mourning," *American Imago* 24 (1967): 248–70; and Thomas J. Stavola, *Scott Fitzgerald: Crisis in an American Identity* (New York: Barnes and Noble, 1979). Koenigsberg, 258, and Stavola, 28, refer briefly to the importance of the daughters' deaths.

2. Robert E. Spiller, Willard Thorp, Thomas H. Johnson, Henry Seidel Canby, Richard M. Ludwig, and William M. Gibson, eds. *The Literary History of the United States*, vol. 1, 4th ed. (New York: Macmillan, 1974), 1299.

3. Pamela Boker, *The Grief Taboo in American Literature: Loss and Prolonged Adolescence in Twain, Melville, and Hemingway* (New York: New York University Press, 1996). Interestingly, Boker mentions Hemingway's disgust with Fitzgerald's "Crack-Up" essays, in which Fitzgerald acknowledged his sense of loss (212).

4. Leslie Fiedler, *Love and Death in the American Novel* (New York: Stein and Day, 1960), 312–16; Judith Fetterley, *The Resisting Reader: A Feminist Approach to American Fiction* (Bloomington: Indiana University Press, 1978), 72–100.

5. Some previous critics have begun to address Fitzgerald's interest in "feminine" values, though they confine their discussion, for the most part, to individual works. On *The Great Gatsby*, see Frances Kerr, "Feeling 'Half-Feminine': Modernism and the Politics of Emotion in *The Great Gatsby*," *American Literature* 68 (1996): 405–31; and Patricia Pacey Thornton, "Sexual Roles in *The Great Gatsby*," *English Studies in Canada* 4 (1979): 457–68. On *Tender Is the Night*, see Milton Stern, *The Golden Moment: The Novels of F. Scott Fitzgerald* (Chicago: University of Illinois Press, 1971). Sarah Beebe Fryer, *Fitzgerald's New Women: Harbingers of Change* (Ann Arbor, Michigan: University of Michigan Research Press, 1988), has discussed Fitzgerald's depiction of believable female characters.

6. See, for example, Alan C. Elms, *Uncovering Lives: The Uneasy Alliance of Biography and Psychology* (New York: Oxford UP, 1994).

7. John Bowlby, *Loss: Sadness and Depression*, vol. 3 of *Attachment and Loss* (New York: Basic, 1980).

CHAPTER ONE

1. F. Scott Fitzgerald, *Afternoon of an Author: A Selection of Uncollected Stories and Essays* (New York: Scribner's, 1957), 184.

2. See especially Matthew J. Bruccoli, *Some Sort of Epic Grandeur* (New York: Harcourt, 1981), 13; Scott Donaldson, *Fool for Love: F. Scott Fitzgerald* (New York: Congdon and Weed, 1983), 16–17; James R. Mellow, *Invented Lives: F. Scott and Zelda Fitzgerald* (Boston: Houghton, 1984), 15; and Jeffrey Meyers, *Scott Fitzgerald: A Biography* (New York: Harper, 1994), 5–6. Demonstrating his tendency to provide facts but not analysis, Bruccoli reprints the statement without commenting directly on it, though he does later infer that Fitzgerald's mother feared he would become the third child in the family to die. Mellow implies that Fitzgerald may have been resorting to self-dramatization in making the statement, since he writes that Fitzgerald "publicly, at least," attempted to make "something mythic" out of the circumstances surrounding his birth. Mellow does feel, though, that the sisters' deaths bore some actual importance in Fitzgerald's life, for he sees a link between Fitzgerald's mother's grief and her pampering of him. This connection is also made by Donaldson, who depicts Fitzgerald's relationship with his mother more vividly than other biographers, and by Meyers. The latter of the two also writes that the deaths similarly "strengthened the bond" between Scott and his father. Moreover, Meyers provides a brief interpretation of Fitzgerald's statement: "[H]e probably meant that he had been born out of suffering, had been singled out for a special survivor's fate, and had been made to feel that his life was particularly precious. His existence somehow had to compensate for their absence" (5–6). This last view is the closest to my own, though Meyers does not provide support for his hypothesis.

3. Sigmund Freud, "The Uncanny," *The Standard Edition of the Complete Works of Sigmund Freud*, trans. and ed. James Strachey, vol. 17 (London: Hogarth, 1978).

4. Ibid., 235.

5. Ibid.

6. Albert C. Cain and Barbara S. Cain, "On Replacing a Child," *Journal of the American Academy of Child Psychiatry* 3 (1964): 443–56.

7. Ibid., 451.

8. Elva Orlow Poznanski, "The 'Replacement Child': A Saga of Unresolved Parental Grief," *Behavioral Pediatrics* 81 (1972): 1190–93.

9. Vamik D. Volkan, *Linking Objects and Linking Phenomena: A Study of the Forms, Symptoms, Metapsychology, and Therapy of Complicated Mourning* (New York: International University Press, 1981), 321; John Bowlby, *Loss: Sadness and Depression* (New York: Basic, 1980).

10. Volkan, *Linking Objects*, 104–5.

11. Ibid., 318.

12. Ibid., 321.

13. Ibid., 347.

14. Vamik D. Volkan, "Becoming a Psychoanalyst," *Analysts at Work: Practice, Principles, and Techniques*, ed. Joseph Reppen (New York: Analytic Press, 1985), 215–31.

15. Jules Glenn, "Twinship Themes and Fantasies in the Work of Thornton Wilder," *Psychoanalytic Study of the Child* 41 (1986): 627–51.

16. George H. Pollock, "Bertha Pappenheim's Pathological Mourning: Possible Effects of Childhood Sibling Loss," *Journal of the American Psychoanalytic Association* 20 (1972): 476–93.

17. Bowlby, *Loss*, 356–70.

18. Ibid., 222–23.

19. Ibid., 223.

20. Ibid., 219–20.

21. Stanley L. Olinick, *The Psychotherapeutic Instrument* (New York: Jason Aronson, 1980), 12–13.

22. Ibid., 160.

23. Bowlby, *Loss*, 333–37.

24. Heinz Kohut, *The Analysis of the Self* (New York: International University Press, 1981).

25. F. Scott Fitzgerald, *The Apprentice Fiction of F. Scott Fitzgerald, 1909–1917*, ed. John Kuehl (Rahway: Rutgers University Press, 1965) 178.

26. F. Scott Fitzgerald, *The Letters of F. Scott Fitzgerald*, ed. Andrew Turnbull (New York: Scribner's, 1963), 419. Subsequent references to this edition, abbreviated LFSF, are provided in parentheses in this chapter.

27. F. Scott Fitzgerald, *F. Scott Fitzgerald's Ledger: A Facsimile* (Washington, D. C. NCR / Microcard, 1972). On boy's clothing around the turn of the century, see Kenneth Lynn, *Hemingway* (New York: Simon, 1987), 38–40. Of possible relevance here is Fitzgerald's self-acknowledged "Freudian complex"—his lifelong fear of showing his feet to others—as well as the occasion on which he joyfully posed in drag for a publicity photograph for Princeton's theatrical club.

28. Bruccoli, *Epic Grandeur*, 14.

29. Fitzgerald, *Ledger*, 154.

30. Qtd. in Donaldson, *Fool for Love*, 16.

31. Andrew Turnbull, *Scott Fitzgerald* (New York: Scribner's, 1962), 7.

32. Qtd. in Donaldson, *Fool for Love*, 16.

33. F. Scott Fitzgerald, *The Price Was High: The Last Uncollected Stories of F. Scott Fitzgerald*, ed. Matthew J. Bruccoli (New York: Harcourt, 1979), 738–39.

34. Ann Douglas, *Terrible Honesty: Mongrel Manhattan in the 1920s* (New York: Farrar, 1995) uses the term "matricidal" in describing the antifeminist nature of modernist American culture.

35. See, for example, Bowlby, *Loss*, chapter 14.

36. Qtd. in Bruccoli, *Epic Grandeur*, 19.

37. Fitzgerald, *Ledger*, 160.

38. Fitzgerald, *Afternoon of an Author*, 185.

39. Joan M. Allen, *Candles and Carnival Lights: The Catholic Sensibility of F. Scott Fitzgerald* (New York: New York University Press, 1978), 64–66, refers to Freud's theory of the family romance.

40. Sigmund Freud, *The Standard Edition of the Complete Psychological Works of Sigmund Freud*, trans. and ed. James Strachey, vol. 9 (London: Hogarth, 1978), 237–38. It is worth considering Freud's theory in relation to Jay Gatsby's mysterious past. Like his creator, Gatsby came to believe as a child that he was not the son of his parents. Did a feeling of being underloved contribute to Gatsby's changeling fantasy? If so, does his immense desire for Daisy stem in part from a latent need for parental love? See my discussion in chapter five of Daisy's role as a preoccupied mother.

41. Qtd. in Turnbull, *Fitzgerald*, 259.

42. F. Scott Fitzgerald, *Correspondence of F. Scott Fitzgerald*, ed. Matthew J. Bruccoli and Margaret M. Duggan (New York: Random House, 1980), 421–22.

43. Fitzgerald, *Apprentice Fiction*, 178.

44. F. Scott Fitzgerald, *The Crack-Up with Other Pieces and Stories* (Middlesex, U. K.: Penguin, 1987), 48.

45. Ibid., 52.

46. Ibid., 33.

47. Ibid., 53.

48. Fitzgerald, *Correspondence*, 398.

49. Turnbull, *Fitzgerald*, 220.

50. Sheilah Graham and Gerold Frank, *Beloved Infidel: The Education of a Woman* (New York: Henry Holt, 1958), 247.

51. Qtd. in Donaldson, *Fool for Love*, 56.

52. Meyers, *Biography*, 42.

53. Graham and Frank, *Beloved Infidel*, 242.

54. Fitzgerald, *Correspondence*, 61.

55. Zelda Fitzgerald, *The Collected Writings*, ed. Matthew J. Bruccoli (New York: Scribner's, 1991), 10.

56. Ibid.

57. Ibid.

58. Qtd. in Lynn, *Hemingway*, 287.

59. Ibid.

60. Fitzgerald, *Afternoon of an Author*, 185.

61. Turnbull, *Fitzgerald*, 198.

62. F. Scott Fitzgerald, *The Notebooks of F. Scott Fitzgerald*, ed. Matthew J. Bruccoli (New York: Harcourt, 1978), 159.

CHAPTER TWO

1. Andrew Turnbull, *Scott Fitzgerald* (New York, Scribner's, 1962), 199.

2. Ibid.

3. Ibid.

4. F. Scott Fitzgerald, *The Stories of F. Scott Fitzgerald*, ed. Malcolm Cowley (New York: Scribner's Classic, 1986), 410. Subsequent references to this edition, abbreviated SFSF, are provided in parentheses.

5. It is not certain that Stella has actually had a baby. We never see her baby in the story, and Stella does not respond directly to Joel's question about whether she is a recent mother. It is possible that his question is wildly inappropriate, a reflection of his inner concern with the preoccupied mother of his childhood. Since Miles now ignores Stella sexually, he may have done so from the beginning of their marriage. However, it is more likely that she does not respond to Joel's question about her motherhood because he knows she has a child and asks the question rhetorically.

6. Kenneth G. Johnston, "Fitzgerald's 'Crazy Sunday': Cinderella in Hollywood," *Literature / Film Quarterly* 6 (1978): 214–21.

7. Jeffrey Berman, *The Talking Cure: Literary Representations of Psychoanalysis* (New York: New York University Press, 1985), 79.

8. In the beginning of the story, Fitzgerald refers to the "money men" (Jews) who run Hollywood. In *The Notebooks of F. Scott Fitzgerald*, ed. Matthew J. Bruccoli (New York: Harcourt, 1978), 318, Fitzgerald uses a similar phrase, referring to a woman he knew who accidentally insulted "those finance-Jews." In keeping with Jewish conspiracy theories, the "money men" in "Crazy Sunday" eventually seem like a wrathful, exclusionary cabal. In Joel's sketch, he parodies someone with a Jewish-sounding name—Dave Silverstein—and the partygoers, the members of the "clan," shrink from him, as if they are afraid of reprisal if they show support for his criticism of a Jew. During Joel's sketch, they crowded around him in a "sinister Indian-like half-circle"—another suggestion of ethnic conflict. In admiring Calman's ability to take heed of his own artistic sensibility, Joel admires someone with a Christian-sounding name who has managed to avoid being silenced. Thus, while it is unclear in the story whether or not Stella is the "good" parent among the "clan," the money men are certainly the "bad" parents. We find that, in an unsettling reversal, the Jews have become the counterpart to blueblooded, exclusionary Americans such as Tom and Daisy Buchanan in *The Great Gatsby*. In contrast, the paternalistic Jewish characters Bloeckman in *The Beautiful and Damned* and Stahr in *The Last Tycoon* do not exclude others. Rather, they care for those less fortunate than themselves.

9. F. Scott Fitzgerald, *Six Tales of the Jazz Age and Other Stories* (New York: Scribner's, 1960), 145.

10. Christiane Johnson, "Freedom, Contingency, and Ethics in 'The Adjuster,' " in *The Short Stories of F. Scott Fitzgerald: New Approaches in Criticism*, ed. Jackson R. Bryer (Madison: University of Wisconsin Press, 1982), 229.

11. Fitzgerald, *Jazz Age*, 154. Johnson has previously made clear tht Dr. Moon represents time.

12. Ibid., 159.

13. Johnson, 237–38.

14. Johnson, 239, observes that Luella's adjustment to loss is "not very convincing."

15. Fitzgerald, *Jazz Age*, 157.

16. Edwin Moses, "F. Scott Fitzgerald and the Quest for the Ice Palace," *CEA Critic* 36.2 (1974): 12; Alice Hall Petry, *Fitzgerald's Craft of Short Fiction: The Collected Stories, 1920–1935* (Ann Arbor: University of Michigan Research Press, 1989): 46.

CHAPTER THREE

1. F. Scott Fitzgerald, *This Side of Paradise*, ed. James L. W. West III (New York: Cambridge University Press, 1995), 215–16. Subsequent references to this edition, abbreviated TSOP, are provided in parentheses.

2. See, for example, Sergio Perosa, *The Art of F. Scott Fitzgerald*, trans. Charles Matz and Perosa (Ann Arbor: University of Michigan Press, 1965); and Richard D. Lehan, *F. Scott Fitzgerald and the Craft of Fiction* (Carbondale: Southern Illinois University Press, 1966), 72–73.

3. F. Scott Fitzgerald, *The Letters of F. Scott Fitzgerald*, ed. Andrew Turnbull (New York: Scribner's, 1963), 468–69.

4. John Bowlby, *Loss: Sadness and Depression*, vol. 3 of *Attachment and Loss* (New York: Basic, 1980). For a related discussion of narcissism in the novel, see Madelyn Hoffman, "*This Side of Paradise*: A Study in Pathological Narcissism," *Literature and Psychology* 28 (1978): 178–85. Hoffman does not relate her discussion to the issue of maternal depression. An appreciation of the depression that hinders Beatrice's parenting allows us to become resisting feminist readers, for we can then oppose her son's callous attitude toward her.

5. Martha Wolfenstein has suggested that because of the environmental changes occurring during adolescence, this stage is better suited than previous stages for the child's development of the capacity to mourn. See "How is Mourning Possible?" *Psychoanalytic Study of the Child* 21 (1966): 91–123; and "Loss, Rage, and Repetition," *Psychoanalytic Study of the Child* 24 (1969): 432–60.

6. Sigmund Freud, "Mourning and Melancholia," *The Standard Edition of the Complete Works of Sigmund Freud*, trans. and ed. James Strachey, vol. 14 (London: Hogarth, 1978).

7. Fitzgerald, *Letters*, 602.

CHAPTER FOUR

1. F. Scott Fitzgerald, *The Beautiful and Damned* (New York: Scribner's, 1995), 76. Subsequent references to this edition, abbreviated BD, are provided in parentheses.

2. James E. Miller, Jr., *The Fictional Technique of Scott Fitzgerald* (The Hague: Martinus Nijhoff, 1957), 53, 59.

3. Henry Dan Piper, *F. Scott Fitzgerald: A Critical Portrait* (Carbondale: Southern Illinois University Press, 1968), 92.

4. Ibid.

5. Sigmund Freud, "The Uncanny," *The Standard Edition of the Complete Works of Sigmund Freud*, trans. and ed. James Strachey, vol. 17 (London: Hogarth, 1978), 241.

6. Hinduism's theory of reincarnation influenced both theosophy and Buddhism. Note that "Bilphism" sounds like "Buddhism."

7. My views on Fitzgerald's depiction of Bloeckman's Jewishness were informed by a conference paper by Barry Gross of Michigan State University. For an alternative view on the question of anti-Semitism in the novel, see for example, Jeffrey Meyers, *Scott Fitzgerald: A Biography* (New York: Harper, 1994), 329.

Readers of the novel may note that Fitzgerald sometimes undercuts his attempt, through the narrator, to condemn bigotry. For example, when Maury waxes philosophical in professing his nihilistic theories, decrying the fact that he sees in America "the black beginning to mingle with the white" (255), his sentiment is not viewed critically by the narrator, who "steps aside" throughout Maury's reactionary diatribe. Moreover, readers of the novel might argue that in lauding Bloeckman's self-conscious courteousness, the narrator is approving of Bloeckman only because of his desire to assimilate. It is true that the novel does not endorse diversity, and the same could be said of *The Last Tycoon*, where Stahr's Jewishness is not depicted. My aim in the body of this chapter is simply to point out that Fitzgerald is aware of Anthony's unfairness to Bloeckman and that he intentionally delineates the psychology behind it.

    8. For a discussion of the ambiguity of the ending, including a summary of previous critics' views, see Miller, *Fictional Technique*, 58–59.

    9. F. Scott Fitzgerald, *The Letters of F. Scott Fitzgerald*, ed. Andrew Turnbull (New York, Scribner's, 1963), 478.

CHAPTER FIVE

    1. F. Scott Fitzgerald, *The Great Gatsby*, ed. Matthew J. Bruccoli (New York: Cambridge University Press, 1991), 140. Subsequent references to this edition, abbreviated GG, are provided in parentheses.

    2. A. B. Paulson, "Oral Aggression and Splitting," in *Modern Critical Interpretations: F. Scott Fitzgerald's* The Great Gatsby, ed. Harold Bloom (New York: Chelsea, 1986).

    3. Vamik D. Volkan, *Linking Objects and Linking Phenomena: A Study of the Forms, Symptoms, Metapsychology, and Therapy of Complicated Mourning* (New York: International University Press, 1981).

    4. Patricia Pacey Thornton, "Sexual Roles in *The Great Gatsby*," *English Studies in Canada* 4 (1979): 457–68, discusses Nick's embracing of sympathy and caring, qualities traditionally associated with women. Though Thornton's argument is insightful, it is difficult to accept a central view of hers: that Nick is the "ideal" sympathizer for Gatsby, Daisy, Jordan, Myrtle, and Catherine (Myrtle's sister). Except for Gatsby, these characters seem to receive only a limited sympathy, if any at all, from Nick. If we focus more upon the importance of another form of caring in the novel—caring for the dead / absent—we can better appreciate Nick's difference from other more "masculine" characters in the novel and also better understand the essence of Gatsby's greatness. In "Feeling 'Half-Feminine': Modernism and the Politics of Emotion in *The Great Gatsby*," *American Literature* 68 (1996): 405–431, Frances Kerr finds Fitzgerald to be contradictory in his presentation of "feminine" emotionality in the novel. My argument partially accords with Kerr's, for I discuss Nick's ambivalence toward "feminine" mourning. However, in arguing that Nick ultimately overcomes his negativity, I provide a contrasting argument.

    5. While working on the final typescript of this book, I discovered Mitch Breitwieser's "*The Great Gatsby*: Grief, Jazz, and the Eye-Witness," *Arizona Quarterly* 47 (1991): 17–70. Breitwieser's discussion has little in common with my own, though he does similarly propose that the halting of the train by the valley of ashes is a symbol of halted grief.

    6. R. Laurence Moore, "The Medium and Her Message," in *In Search of White Crows: Spiritualism, Parapsychology, and American Culture* (New York: 0xford University Press, 1977).

7. The word "ectoplasm" also suggests raciness, since it was said that the ectoplasm usually emanated from the medium's genitals.

8. Keath Fraser, "Another Reading of *The Great Gatsby*," *Interpretations*, ed. Bloom. See also Kerr, Edward Wasiolek, "The Sexual Drama of Nick and Gatsby," *The International Fiction Review* 19 (1992): 14–22, who discuss the novel's homoeroticism as well.

9. In writing this passage, Fitzgerald appropriated his wife's words upon the birth of their daughter. It is worth noting that in transposing Zelda's words, Fitzgerald added a reference to the one-hour time period and to the sex of the child. His concern with the sex of Daisy's child is interesting in light of his parents' tragic experiences with three of the four daughters born to them. And his reference to the one-hour time period reminds us of the entry in his ledger about the death of his parents' third daughter: "His mother presented him with a sister who lived only an hour." See *F. Scott Fitzgerald's Ledger: A Facsimile* (Washington, D.C.: National Congressional Record, 1972), 154.

10. Given my argument about the importance of parental grief in the novel, it is also worth noting one of Fitzgerald's "slips" in writing it. In the original published version, Fitzgerald had Daisy state that Pammy is three years old (an error that has been corrected in the Cambridge edition). This would mean that Pammy was conceived before Daisy's marriage, which Fitzgerald must not have "intended" to indicate. Since Pammy's birth seems to lie very near the heart of Daisy's depression, more so even than her relationship to Tom, it seems appropriate in a sense that in the original published version, her grief over Pammy's birth arose prior to her unfortunate marriage.

11. F. Scott Fitzgerald, *The Letters of F. Scott Fitzgerald*, ed. Andrew Turnbull (New York: Scribner's, 1963), 602, refers to Little Eva, Topsy's white double in *Uncle Tom's Cabin*.

CHAPTER SIX

1. Jeffrey Berman, *The Talking Cure: Literary Representations of Psychoanalysis* (New York: New York University Press, 1985), 77, 72.

2. Vamik D. Volkan, *Linking Objects and Linking Phenomena: A Study of the Forms, Symptoms, Metapsychology, and Therapy of Complicated Mourning* (New York: International University Press, 1981).

3. Berman, *Talking Cure*, 66.

4. Elaine Showalter, *The Female Malady* (New York: Pantheon, 1985), 191.

5. F. Scott Fitzgerald, *Tender Is the Night* (New York, Scribner's, 1982), 81. Subsequent references to this edition, abbreviated TITN, are provided in parentheses.

6. Fitzgerald likely had in mind here the death of Zelda's brother shortly before her birth. Because I feel that a consideration of Fitzgerald's childhood will be more useful to our understanding of Nicole's "schizophrenia" than an analysis of Zelda's background, I avoid drawing parallels between Zelda and Nicole elsewhere in this chapter.

7. Aware that the plot of the initial draft of the novel was entitled "The Boy Who Killed His Mother," Berman (*Talking Cure*) and other critics have explored the "matricidal" aspect of the final draft. Judith Fetterley, "Who Killed Dick Diver? The Sexual Politics of *Tender Is the Night*," *Mosaic* 17 (1984): 111–28, has previously discussed Fitzgerald's criticism of the feminization of American culture, as I do here. However, she does not investigate the ways in which Fitzgerald sincerely defends nineteenth-century feminist values, as I do in this chapter. In contrast, Milton R. Stern, *The Golden Moment: The Novels of F. Scott Fitzgerald* (Chicago: University of Illinois Press, 1971), discusses the "feminine" element in the novel but does not explore the misogyny. In stressing the lifelong nature of Fitzgerald's / Dick's ambivalence toward femininity, I suggest that both the positive and negative sides of that ambivalence lie deep within their psyches and therefore should be considered alongside of each other.

8. Perhaps also relevantly, Lincoln was a doting father—behavior unusual for a man in his time—and he and his wife were devastated by the loss of two of their sons. One son died while Lincoln was president.

9. Berman, *Talking Cure*, 67.

10. Ibid., 72.

11. Ibid.

12. Given these parallels, we can infer one reason why Fitzgerald based Rosemary's character on the autobiographically named character Francis from an earlier version of the novel, while Baby Warren is based upon Francis's mother. See Matthew J. Bruccoli, *The Composition of* Tender Is the Night: *A Study of the Manuscripts* (Pittsburgh: University of Pittsburgh Press, 1963), 95.

The predicament of the living linking object, and also the issues of transference and countertransference in the novel, illuminate the disagreement between Fitzgerald and Hemingway over the use of "composite characters." Hemingway felt that Fitzgerald should not have combined autobiographical qualities with those of Gerald Murphy in delineating Dick's character, and he objected to other characters on similar grounds. However, Fitzgerald's focus on the predicament of the living linking object and transference love lends itself to his creation of characters who have multiple sides to their personalities.

13. For example, Matthew J. Bruccoli, *Some Sort of Epic Grandeur: The Life of F. Scott Fitzgerald* (New York: Harcourt, 1981), 341 notes that Dick Diver is a slang term for the act of fellatio; Berman, *Talking Cure*, 81, notes the phallic connotation of the words Dick repeats to himself—"Lucky Dick, you big stiff" (114)—and also refers to the symbolic castration that occurs when Dick's nose is broken by a policeman; and Leslie Fiedler, *Love and Death in the American Novel* (New York: Stein and Day, 1960), 301–2, refers to Dick's donning of "lace panties," and the presence of several homosexual characters who "haunt" the novel. All of these details illuminate Fitzgerald's / Dick's homophobia.

14. See Ann Douglas, *The Feminization of American Culture* (New York: Knopf, 1977).

15. Showalter, *Female Malady*, 167–68.

16. F. Scott Fitzgerald, *The Letters of F. Scott Fitzgerald*, ed. Andrew Turnbull (New York: Scribner's, 1963), 247.

17. Just as Dick perverts his father's moral code in becoming entangled with his patient in the Mount Chillon episode, the Chilean character Francisco rebels against his father by engaging in homosexual behavior. Note Fitzgerald's use of an autobiographical name for this character, as well as the Chillon-Chilean pun.

18. Berman, *Talking Cure*, 82–83.

19. On Fitzgerald's use of oral imagery in the novel, see Thomas J. Stavola, *Crisis in an American Identity* (New York: Barnes and Noble, 1979). We recollect the oral image I cited previously of Nicole sucking on Dick's lean chest.

20. Possibly as well, an element of survivor guilt is reflected in Fitzgerald's portrayal of Dick's self-destructiveness. Fitzgerald refers directly in the novel to characters experiencing a sense of inferiority or subservience to their relatives. Franz's desire to follow in the footsteps of forefathers is tamed by his belief that he can never attain their greatness. He admits that he finds it "difficult" to be ambitious when he must repeatedly pass the statue commemorating a famous relative, as well as the cemeteries where his many renowned ancestors are buried. One of Dick's patients pretends she can play a musical instrument so that she can appear as accomplished as her two sisters, who are both "brilliant" musicians. Mary North's two sisters-in-law from her second marriage, in accordance with their Himadoun tradition, become ladies-in-waiting to Mary, because she is their brother's wife. The sisters-in-law thus devote their lives to their sibling. Perhaps, then, like these characters, Dick feels survivor guilt, a sense that the sisters whom his parents mourned for were superior to him, that they should have lived instead of him. It is true that he associates survivorship with guilt, for when Nicole tells him that her family regained its wealth after her grandmother's death, he says that he forgives her, as if imagining that she wished for the death and inheritance. As someone fascinated with the lives of the romantic poets, Fitzgerald would likely have known that Keats had lost a brother shortly before writing the poem referred to in the title of Fitzgerald's novel. Writing of the self-destructive fantasy embedded within "Ode to a Nightingale," Helen Vendler, *The Odes of John Keats* (Cambridge, Massachusetts: Harvard University Press, 1983), 83 notes that Keats's "guilt as a survivor of his brother's death and his sense of the pain of the world around him pressed him toward silence and suicide." Though the novel does not contain an allusion to Keats's experience with sibling loss, Fitzgerald does allude to Keats's early death in order to foreshadow his protagonist's early demise. When Dick visits the home where Keats died, his "spirit soar[s]," as if he senses a kindred spirit.

21. John Bowlby, *Loss: Sadness and Depression*, vol. 3 of *Attachment and Loss* (New York: Basic, 1980), 343–44, 346–47; and Erwin Stengel, "Studies on the Psychopathology of Compulsive Wandering," *The British Journal of Medical Psychology* 18 (1941): 250–51 discuss the connection between compulsive wandering and parental loss in childhood.

22. Interestingly, in writing to John Peale Bishop about the understated style of the novel, Fitzgerald (*Letters*), 363), reveals his anxiety over the debilitating, "shell shocking" effects of emotion upon his reader. He writes that "there were moments all through the book where I could have pointed up dramatic scenes, and I *deliberately* refrained from doing so because the ma-

terial itself was so harrowing and highly charged that I did not want to subject the reader to a series of nervous shocks in a novel that was inevitably close to whoever read it in my generation."

CHAPTER SEVEN

1. Melanie Klein, *Contributions to Psycho-Analysis, 1921–1945* (London: Hogarth, 1950), posits that when adults face loss, they regress to the "depressive position" initially brought on by their experience with maternal loss. Thus, Klein's theory would suggest that Fitzgerald's grief as an adult would give rise to his sense of loss as an infant, his need to face ambivalence toward his mother and father as well, since the latter played an important role in his infancy. In other words, his need to modulate his good and bad "internal objects," as Klein puts it. Increasingly, feminist theorists stress that the child's maturation involves not only less polarized views of the mother as object, but also an acceptance of the mother's subjectivity. See, for example, Nancy J. Chodorow, *Feminism and Psychoanalytic Theory* (New Haven: Yale University Press, 1989); ed. Bassin, Margaret Horney, and Meryle Mahrer Kaplan, "Maternal Subjectivity in the Culture of Nostalgia: Mourning and Memory," *Representations of Motherhood*, ed. Margaret Horney Bassin and Meryle Mahrer Kaplan (New Haven: Yale University Press, 1994). In accepting his parents as complex people faced with difficult choices in difficult circumstances, Fitzgerald would have been accepting both their objectivity and subjectivity.

My use of the description "good-enough" comes from D. W. Winnicott, *Playing and Reality* (New York: Basic, 1971).

2. F. Scott Fitzgerald, *The Love of the Last Tycoon: A Western*, ed. Matthew J. Bruccoli (New York: Cambridge University Press, 1994), 146. Under the abbreviation LT, all references to Fitzgerald's synopsis, notes, and novel in this edition will be provided in parentheses.

3. John F. Callahan, *The Illusions of a Nation: Myth and History in the Novels of F. Scott Fitzgerald* (Urbana: University of Illinois Press, 1972), 208, also contrasts Gatsby's idealization of Daisy with Stahr's attitude toward Kathleen.

4. Matthew J. Bruccoli, *Some Sort of Epic Grandeur: The Life of F. Scott Fitzgerald* (New York: Harcourt, 1981), 473.

5. F. Scott Fitzgerald, *The Price Was High: The Last Uncollected Stories of F. Scott Fitzgerald*, ed. Matthew J. Bruccoli (New York: Harcourt, 1979), 773.

6. See Leslie Fiedler, *Love and Death in the American Novel* (New York: Stein and Day, 1960).

7. As narrator, Cecilia would be another empathic character. She can appreciate Stahr's grief, for she is in the late stages of the mourning process, seemingly a little ahead of Stahr. She feels "somewhat solemn and subdued" (4) when she thinks of her sister, who died a few years ago. A boyfriend of hers also died some time previously.

8. Callahan, *Illusions of a Nation*, 207.

9. Winnicott, *Playing and Reality*, 25.

10. Vamik D. Volkan, *Linking Objects and Linking Phenomena: A Study of the Forms, Symptoms, Metapsychology, and Therapy of Complicated Mourning* (New York: International University Press, 1981), 373.

11. F. Scott Fitzgerald, *The Notebooks of F. Scott Fitzgerald*, ed. Matthew J. Bruccoli (New York: Harcourt, 1978), 159.

12. F. Scott Fitzgerald, "Echoes of the Jazz Age," *The Crack-Up with Other Pieces and Stories* (London: Penguin, 1987), 9.

Works Cited

Literature, Letters, and Notebooks

Fitzgerald, F. Scott. *Afternoon of an Author: A Selection of Uncollected Stories and Essays*. New York: Scribner's, 1957.

———. *The Apprentice Fiction of F. Scott Fitzgerald, 1909–1917*. Edited by John Kuehl. Rahway: Rutgers University Press, 1965.

———. *The Beautiful and Damned*. New York: Scribner's, 1995.

———. *Correspondence of F. Scott Fitzgerald*. Edited by Matthew J. Bruccoli and Margaret Duggan. New York: Random House, 1980.

———. *The Crack-Up with Other Pieces and Stories*. Middlesex, U. K.: Penguin, 1987.

———. *F. Scott Fitzgerald's Ledger: A Facsimile*. Washington: NCR / Microcard, 1972.

———. *The Letters of F. Scott Fitzgerald*. Edited by Andrew Turnbull. New York: Scribner's, 1963.

———. *The Love of the Last Tycoon: A Western*. Edited by Matthew J. Bruccoli. New York: Cambridge University Press, 1994.

———. *The Notebooks of F. Scott Fitzgerald*. Edited by Matthew J. Bruccoli. New York: Harcourt, 1978.

———. *The Price Was High: The Last Uncollected Stories of F. Scott Fitzgerald*. Edited by Matthew J. Bruccoli. New York: Harcourt, 1979.

———. *Six Tales of the Jazz Age and Other Stories*. New York: Scribner's, 1960.

———. *The Stories of F. Scott Fitzgerald*. Edited by Malcolm Cowley. New York: Scribner Classic, 1986.

———. *Tender Is the Night*. New York: Scribner's, 1982.

———. *This Side of Paradise*. Edited by James L. W. West III. New York: Cambridge University Press, 1995.

Fitzgerald, Zelda. *Collected Writings*. Edited by Matthew J. Bruccoli. New York: Scribner's, 1991.

Biographies, Literary Criticism, and Cultural History

Allen, Joan M. *Candles and Carnival Lights: The Catholic Sensibility of F. Scott Fitzgerald*. New York: New York University Press, 1978.

169

Berman, Jeffrey. *The Talking Cure: Literary Representations of Psychoanalysis*. New York: New York University Press, 1985.

Boker, Pamela. *The Grief Taboo in American Literature: Loss and Prolonged Adolescence in Twain, Melville, and Hemingway*. New York: New York University Press, 1996.

Breitwieser, Mitch. "*The Great Gatsby*: Grief, Jazz, and the Eye-Witness." *Arizona Quarterly* 47 (1991): 17–70.

Bruccoli, Matthew J. *The Composition of* Tender Is the Night: *A Study of the Manuscripts*. Pittsburgh: Pittsburgh Press, 1963.

———. *Some Sort of Epic Grandeur*. New York: Harcourt, 1981.

Callahan, John F. *The Illusions of a Nation: Myth and History in the Novels of F. Scott Fitzgerald*. Urbana: University of Illinois Press, 1972.

Donaldson, Scott. *Fool for Love: F. Scott Fitzgerald*. New York: Congdon and Weed, 1983.

Douglas, Ann. *The Feminization of American Culture*. New York: Knopf, 1977.

———. *Terrible Honesty: Mongrel Manhattan in the 1920s*. New York: Farrar, 1995.

Elms, Alan C. *Uncovering Lives: The Uneasy Alliance of Biography and Psychology*. New York: Oxford University Press, 1994.

Fetterley, Judith. *The Resisting Reader: A Feminist Approach to American Fiction*. Bloomington: Indiana University Press, 1978.

———. "Who Killed Dick Diver? The Sexual Politics of *Tender Is the Night*." *Mosaic* 17 (1984): 111–28

Fiedler, Leslie. *Love and Death in the American Novel*. New York: Stein and Day, 1960.

Fraser, Keath. "Another Reading of *The Great Gatsby*." In *Modern Critical Interpretations: F. Scott Fitzgerald's The Great Gatsby*, edited by Harold Bloom. New York: Chelsea, 1986.

Fryer, Sarah Beebe. *Fitzgerald's New Woman: Harbingers of Change*. Ann Arbor Michigan: University of Michigan Research Press, 1998.

Graham, Sheilah, and Gerold Frank. *Beloved Infidel: The Education of a Woman*. New York: Henry Holt, 1958.

Hoffman, Madelyn. "*This Side of Paradise*: A Study in Pathological Narcissism." *Literature and Psychology* 28 (1978): 178–85.

Holland, Norman N. *The I*. New Haven: Yale University Press, 1985.

Johnson, Christiane. "Freedom, Contingency, and Ethics in 'The Adjuster.' " *The Short Stories of F. Scott Fitzgerald: New Approaches in Criticism*, edited by Jackson R. Bryer. Madison: University of Wisconsin Press, 1982.

Johnston, Kenneth G. "Fitzgerald's 'Crazy Sunday': Cinderella in Hollywood" *Literature / Film Quarterly* 6 (1978): 214–21.

Kerr, Frances. "Feeling 'Half-Feminine': Modernism and the Politics of Emotion in The*Great Gatsby*." *American Literature* 68 (1996): 405–31.

Koenigsberg, Richard A. "F. Scott Fitzgerald: Literature and the Work of Mourning." *American Imago* 24 (1967): 248–70.

Lehan, Richard D. *F. Scott Fitzgerald and the Craft of Fiction*. Carbondale: Southern Illinois University Press, 1966.

Lynn, Kenneth. *Hemingway*. New York: Simon, 1987.

Mellow, James R. *Invented Lives: F. Scott and Zelda Fitzgerald* Boston: Houghton, 1984.

Meyers, Jeffrey. *Scott Fitzgerald: A Biography*. New York: Harper, 1994.

Miller, James E. Jr. *The Fictional Technique of F. Scott Fitzgerald*. The Hague: Martinus Nijhoff, 1957.

Moore, R. Laurence. "The Medium and Her Message." Chapter 4 in *In Search of White Crows: Spiritualism, Parapsychology, and American Culture*. New York: Oxford University Press, 1977.

Moses, Edwin. "F. Scott Fitzgerald and the Quest for the Ice Palace." *CEA Critic* 36.2 (1974): 11–14.

Paulson, A. B. "Oral Aggression and Splitting." *Modern Critical Interpretations: F. Scott Fitzgerald's* The Great Gatsby, edited by Harold Bloom. New York: Chelsea, 1986.

Perosa, Sergio. *The Art of F. Scott Fitzgerald*. Translated by Charles Matz and Perosa. Ann Arbor: University of Michigan Press, 1965.

Petry, Alice Hall. *Fitzgerald's Craft of Short Fiction: The Collected Stories; 1920–1935*. Ann Arbor: University of Michigan Research Press, 1989.

Piper, Henry Dan. *F. Scott Fitzgerald: A Critical Portrait* Carbondale: Southern Illinois University Press, 1968.

Showalter, Elaine. *The Female Malady*. New York: Pantheon, 1985.

Spiller, Robert, Willard Thorp, Thomas H. Johnson, Henry Seidel Canby, Richard M. Ludwig, and William M. Gibson, eds. *The Literary History of the United States*. Vol. 1, 4th editon. New York: Macmillan, 1974.

Stavola, Thomas J. *Scott Fitzgerald: Crisis in an American Identity*. New York: Barnes and Noble, 1979.

Stern, Milton. *The Golden Moment: The Novels of F. Scott Fitzgerald*. Chicago: University of Illinois Press, 1971.

Thornton, Patricia Pacey. "Sexual Roles in *The Great Gatsby*." *English Studies in Canada* 4 (1979): 457–68.

Turnbull, Andrew. *Scott Fitzgerald*. New York: Scribner's, 1962.

Vendler, Helen. *The Odes of John Keats*. Cambridge, Massachusetts: Harvard University Press, 1983.

Wasiolek, Edward. "The Sexual Drama of Nick and Gatsby." *The International Fiction Review* 19 (1992): 14–22.

PSYCHOANALYSIS

Bassin, Donna. "Maternal Subjectivity in the Culture of Nostalgia: Mourning and Memory." In *Representations of Motherhood*, edited by Bassin, Margaret Horney, and Meryle Mahrer Kaplan. New Haven: Yale University Press, 1994.

Bowlby, John. *Loss: Sadness and Depression.* Vol. 3 of *Attachment and Loss.* New York: Basic, 1980.

Cain, Albert C., and Barbara S. Cain. "On Replacing a Child." *Journal of the American Academy of Child Psychiatry* 3 (1964): 443–56.

Chodorow, Nancy. *Feminism and Psychoanalytic Theory.* New Haven: Yale University Press, 1989.

Freud, Sigmund. "Family Romances." *The Standard Edition of the Complete Works of Sigmund Freud.* Translated and edited by James Strachey. Vol. 9. London: Hogarth, 1978.

———. "Mourning and Melancholia." *The Standard Edition of the Complete Works of Sigmund Freud.* Translated and edited by James Strachey. Vol. 14. London: Hogarth, 1978.

———. "The Uncanny." *The Standard Edition of the Complete Works of Sigmund Freud.* Translated and edited by James Strachey. Vol. 17. London: Hogarth, 1978.

Glenn, Jules. "Twinship Themes and Fantasies in the Work of Thornton Wilder." *Psychoanalytic Study of the Child* 41 (1986): 627–51.

Klein, Melanie. *Contributions to Psycho-Analysis, 1921–1945.* London: Hogarth, 1950.

Kohut, Heinz. *The Analysis of the Self.* New York: International University Press, 1981.

Olinick, Stanley L. *The Psychotherapeutic Instrument.* New York: Jason Aronson, 1980.

Pollock, George H. "Bertha Pappenheim's Pathological Mourning: Possible Effects of Childhood Sibling Loss." *Journal of the American Psychoanalytic Association* 20 (1972): 476–93.

Poznanski, Elva Orlow. "The 'Replacement Child': A Saga of Unresolved Parental Grief." *Behavioral Pediatrics* 81 (1972): 1190–93.

Stengel, Erwin. "Studies on the Psychopathology of Compulsive Wandering." *The British Journal of Medical Psychology* 18 (1941): 250–51.

Volkan, Vamik D. "Becoming a Psychoanalyst." In *Analysts at Work: Practice, Principles, and Techniques,* edited by Joseph Reppen. New York: Analytic Press, 1985.

———. *Linking Objects and Linking Phenomena: A Study of the Forms, Symptoms, Metapsychology, and Therapy of Complicated Mourning.* New York: International University Press, 1981.

Winnicott, D. W. *Playing and Reality.* New York: Basic, 1971.

Wolfenstein, Martha. "How Is Mourning Possible?" *Psychoanalytic Study of the Child* 21 (1966): 91–123.

———. "Loss, Rage, and Repetition." *Psychoanalytic Study of the Child* 24 (1969): 432–60.

Index